# Ethics Of The Sages

## Pirke Avot—Annotated & Explained

Translation & Annotation By Rabbi Rami Shapiro

16pt

# Copyright Page from the Original Book

*Ethics of the Sages:*
Pirke Avot—*Annotated & Explained*
2006 First Printing
Translation, annotation, and introductory material © 2006 by Rami Shapiro

All rights reserved. No part of this book may be reproduced or transmitted in any form or by any means, electronic or mechanical, including photocopying, recording, or by any information storage and retrieval system, without permission in writing from the publisher.

For information regarding permission to reprint material from this book, please mail or fax your request in writing to SkyLight Paths Publishing, Permissions Department, at the address / fax number listed below, or e-mail your request to permissions@skylightpaths.com.

**Library of Congress Cataloging-in-Publication Data**
Mishnah. Avot.
Ethics of the sages : Pirke Avot—annotated & explained / translation & annotation by Rami Shapiro.
p. cm. — (SkyLight illuminations series)
Includes bibliographical references.
ISBN-13: 978-1-59473-207-2 (quality pbk.)
ISBN-10: 1-59473-207-8 (quality pbk.)
1. Mishnah. Avot—Commentaries. I. Shapiro, Rami M. II. Mishnah. Avot. English. III. Title.
BM506.A2 2006
296.1'234707—dc22

2006023420

10 9 8 7 6 5 4 3 2 1
Manufactured in the United States of America

> SkyLight Paths Publishing is creating a place where people of different spiritual traditions come together for challenge and inspiration, a place where we can help each other understand the mystery that lies at the heart of our existence.
>
> SkyLight Paths sees both believers and seekers as a community that increasingly transcends traditional boundaries of religion and denomination—people wanting to learn from each other, *walking together, finding the way.*

SkyLight Paths, "Walking Together, Finding the Way," and colophon are trademarks of LongHill Partners, Inc., registered in the U.S. Patent and Trademark Office.
*Walking Together, Finding the Way*®
Published by SkyLight Paths Publishing
A Division of LongHill Partners, Inc.
Sunset Farm Offices, Route 4, P.O. Box 237
Woodstock, VT 05091
Tel: (802) 457-4000    Fax: (802) 457-4004
www.skylightpaths.com

# TABLE OF CONTENTS

| | |
|---|---|
| Other books in the SkyLight Illuminations Series | i |
| Introduction | v |
| A Word on Translation | xxiii |
| Biographical Sketches of the Rabbis in Pirke Avot | xxxii |
| Ethics of the Sages | 1 |
|     Prologue1 | 1 |
|     Chapter One | 4 |
|     Chapter Two | 24 |
|     Chapter Three | 46 |
|     Chapter Four | 75 |
|     Chapter Five | 99 |
|     Chapter Six | 133 |
|     Epilogue | 157 |
| Glossary | 159 |
| Suggested Reading | 176 |
| The ethical teachings of the rabbinic sages come to life | 183 |
| Back Cover Material | 189 |

# Other books in the SkyLight Illuminations Series

*Bhagavad Gita: Annotated & Explained*

*The Book of Mormon: Selections Annotated & Explained*

*Dhammapada: Annotated & Explained*

*The Divine Feminine in Biblical Wisdom Literature: Selections Annotated & Explained*

*The End of Days: Essential Selections from Apocalyptic Texts—Annotated & Explained*

*The Gospel of Philip: Annotated & Explained*

*The Gospel of Thomas: Annotated & Explained*

*Hasidic Tales: Annotated & Explained*

*The Hebrew Prophets: Selections Annotated & Explained*

*The Hidden Gospel of Matthew: Annotated & Explained*

*The Lost Sayings of Jesus: Teachings from Ancient Christian, Jewish, Gnostic and Islamic Sources—Annotated & Explained*

*Native American Stories of the Sacred: Annotated & Explained*

*Philokalia: The Eastern Christian Spiritual Texts—Selections Annotated & Explained*

*Rumi and Islam: Selections from His Stories, Poems, and Discourses—Annotated & Explained*

*The Secret Book of John: The Gnostic Gospel—Annotated & Explained*

*Selections from the Gospel of Sri Ramakrishna: Annotated & Explained*

*Spiritual Writings on Mary: Annotated & Explained*

*Tao Te Ching: Annotated & Explained*

*The Way of a Pilgrim: Annotated & Explained*

*Zohar: Annotated & Explained*

My love of *Pirke Avot* comes from my love of the man who first introduced it to me, Dr. Ellis Rivkin of Hebrew Union College. I first heard him at the HUC campus in Jerusalem in the summer of 1975, before I had entered rabbinical school. His teaching opened worlds to me and in me that I never suspected existed in either Judaism or myself. He was my professor, guide, mentor, and friend for the five years of my rabbinic training and has remained all these over the decades since. I don't know if he knows how much he shaped me. I hope this book makes him proud.

# Introduction

*Pirke Avot,* literally "Chapters of the Fathers" but often referred to as "Ethics of the Sages," has been my steady companion for over forty years. I first stumbled across an English translation in the second-floor stacks of Johnson's Used Bookstore in my hometown, Springfield, Massachusetts. I would spend hours sifting through the piles and piles of books and magazines that crammed the shelves and rose in great heaps on the tables that filled this musty loft almost to bursting. It was my Treasure Island, my Magic Kingdom.

I remember finding a copy of Judah Goldin's *Living Talmud,* his translation of *Pirke Avot.* At the time, 1967 or 1968, the book was only four or five years old, but this particular copy was already well worn, with a fractured spine and fraying pages. I was not particularly interested in the Talmud, but something about the book called to me. I bought it and walked to the courthouse steps to sit and read it. It was not my father's Talmud.

Instead of the deep debate and, to me, all-too-legalistic obsessions of the Rabbis, *Pirke Avot* is a compendium of pithy, insightful, and engaging sayings on what matters in life, and how to live it with dignity. While some of the references escaped me, the vast majority of the teachings were clear and compelling. I read the book in no more than an hour or so. I then stuffed it into the back pocket of my Levi's and walked to the bus stop to go home.

As I walked I kept thinking about what I had read. I pulled the book out of my pocket, flipped to the teaching that I was thinking about, and reread it. On second reading I found something more. The same was true on the third and fourth reading as well. As Ben Bag Bag says, "Turn Her and turn Her, for all things are in Her" (5:26). While the "her" refers to Torah, the Five Books of Moses, the same can be said for *Pirke Avot* as well.

I have turned this book over and over, and it never fails to instruct and surprise. I made my first translation, a self-published book called *Teachings,* in the 1980s, and Bell Tower published my

Zen-like interpretive version in 1993. This version you are reading is more accurate, moving my interpretation to the commentary on the facing page.

How I understand what the text says, then, is easily discovered in the pages of translation and commentary. What the text is, why it matters, and what it means is the subject of this short introduction.

## What Is Pirke Avot?

*Pirke Avot* is the ninth of ten tractates found in *Nezikin,* the Book of Damages, which is the fourth volume of the six-volume Mishnah. The Mishnah (from the Hebrew word *shanah,* "to repeat," as in "To repeat what one has learned from one's teacher") is the first authoritative collection of rabbinic teaching. Redacted during the first two decades of the second century CE by Yehudah HaNasi (Judah the Prince, or president of the Sanhedrin, the rabbinic court), material in the Mishnah spans a five-hundred-year period from the scribes in the time of Ezra to the *tannaim* (the early rabbinic sages).

Commentary on the Mishnah by later Rabbis called *amoraim* (from *amar,* "to say or retell"), who lived between 200CE and 500CE in both Israel and Babylonia, is called Gemara (from *gamar,* "to complete"). Together, Mishnah and Gemara compose the Talmud, the "Learning," which is the heart of Rabbinic Judaism.

Unlike the rest of the Mishnah, *Pirke Avot* has no Gemara, no rabbinic amplification by the *amoraim.* And, unlike the rest of the Talmud, *Pirke Avot* lacks any legal or narrative content. It is simply a compendium of sayings primarily dealing with how best to live your life.

Spanning a period from the second century BCE to the second century CE, *Pirke Avot* collects the ethical insights of the five *zugot* (pairs), the leaders of the Sanhedrin, and forty-three sages who came after them. The Sanhedrin, from the Greek *synedrion,* meaning "sitting together," is the seventy-one-member council of Jewish sages. The Sanhedrin was led by a *Nasi* (Prince), who functioned as the president, and an *Av Bet Din* (Father of the Court), who acted as vice president. The sixty-nine additional members sat in a semicircle when debating issues brought before them. The *zugot* comprised a *Nasi* and an *Av Bet Din*. The five *zugot* were as follows:

Yose ben Yoezer and Yose ben Yochanan (prior to 160BCE)

Yehoshua ben Perachyah and Nittai of Arbel (c.130BCE)

Yehudah ben Tabbai and Shimon ben Shatach (c.100–75BCE)

Shemayah and Avtalyon (first century BCE)

Hillel and Shammai (end of first century BCE to just prior to 30CE)

Originally *Pirke Avot* consisted of five chapters. A sixth chapter of post-Mishnaic material was added by Babylonian Jews, who instituted the custom of reading *Pirke Avot* between the festivals of Pesach (Passover; marking the Exodus from Egypt) and Shavuot (marking the giving of the Ten Commandments on Mount Sinai). The sixth chapter, which deals primarily with Torah study, was added as supplementary reading for the Sabbath before Shavuot.

# Why Does Pirke Avot Matter?

The answer to this question is simple: without *Pirke Avot,* Judaism disappears. To be more precise, without the first sentence of *Pirke Avot,* Judaism disappears.

Judaism as we know it, and as Jews have defined and followed it for the past two thousand years, is Rabbinic Judaism. Rabbinic Judaism rests on the notion that the early Rabbis were not simply interpreters of Torah, but recipients of a Torah all their own. Rabbinic Judaism holds that God gave two Torahs to Moses on Mount Sinai: a Written Torah, the Five Books of Moses, which was given to and preserved by the priests with whom the Written Torah is primarily concerned; and an Oral Torah, which elucidates the Written Torah and adds laws and traditions not found in the Written Torah. The Oral Torah was entrusted to the tribal elders and prophets, who passed it on to the Pharisees, the founders of Rabbinic Judaism.

This is a bold claim, and one that the Written Torah itself does not make. In fact there is only one place in the entirety of Jewish literature that the Pharisaic claim is validated, and that is the opening verse of *Pirke Avot:* "Moses received Torah from Sinai and transmitted it to Joshua; Joshua transmitted it to the elders; the elders to the prophets; and the prophets to the sages of the Great Assembly" (*Pirke Avot* 1:1). If this one-sentence history of the revelation on Sinai is true, Rabbinic Judaism stands. If it is false, Rabbinic Judaism—the only Judaism we have known for millennia—collapses under the weight of its own hubris.

Look at the sentence carefully. God transmits Torah to Moses, who then passes it on to ... Joshua? Nowhere in the Bible does it say that Joshua inherits the Torah. On the contrary, the Bible is very clear that it is Aaron and his descendants who are the keepers of the revelation and the sacrificial system it supports. Joshua is the military and secular leader, but Torah belongs to the priests. Yet in *Pirke Avot'*s retelling of the history of revelation, the priests and their Temple are not even mentioned.

The thousand-year reign of the central authority in Jewish life isn't even given a passing nod. Why? Because the authors of *Pirke Avot,* the Pharisees, rooted in the lower and middle classes of Israel, are competing with the Sadducees, the priestly aristocracy, for the loyalty of the people, and the legitimacy of their teaching depends on the authenticity of their claim to be in the direct line of Torah transmission.

The Pharisees evolved from the scribes and scholars who instituted the centrality of Torah during and after the Babylonian exile (fifth century BCE). The Babylonian king Nebuchadnezzar exiled the Judean king Jehoiachin along with ten thousand other Jews in 598BCE and set up Jehoiachin's uncle, Zedekiah, as a puppet ruler over Judah. Zedekiah, however, led a revolt against Babylonian rule that resulted in the sacking of Jerusalem and a second wave of exile in 586BCE (22 Kings 25:8–21).

Exiled in Babylonia, the Jews invented an alternative to Temple worship: they gathered formally, perhaps each Shabbat, to bemoan their fate, pray for their redemption, and hear the law and lore of their people read aloud. This is the origin of the synagogue: "Thus said the Lord God: I have indeed removed them far among the nations, and I have scattered them among the countries, and I have become to them a small sanctuary in the countries to which they have gone" (Ezekiel 11:16). It is also the origin of the Written Torah, the Five Books of Moses.

If the scholars were to explain the Torah to the people, they had to decide what exactly was Torah. Forty years later, when Nebuchadnezzar and Babylon had fallen to the Persian king Cyrus and the Jews were allowed to return to Judah, they seem to have done just that.

Nehemiah 8:1–3 tells us that when the exiles returned to Judah, "the people gathered together as one at the plaza before the Water Gate, and they asked Ezra the Scholar [also called Ezra the *Kohen* or Priest] to bring the scroll of the Torah of Moses, which God had commanded to Israel. So Ezra the *Kohen* brought the Torah before the congregation—men and women, and all those who could listen with understanding—on the first day of the seventh month. He read from it before the plaza that is before the Water Gate from dawn until noon, in front of the men and women and those who understood; and the ears of the people were attentive to the Torah scroll."

The Torah that Ezra read to the people was the Five Books of Moses. The people who could explain to the masses what they were hearing, "those who could listen with understanding," were the scribes and scholars who eventually became the Pharisees. Ezra was chief among these. Described as a "brilliant scholar of Torah" (Ezra 7:6), Ezra devoted himself to expounding the Torah "and to fulfill and teach [its] statute and law in Israel" (Ezra 7:10).

In Hebrew the word "expound" is *li-derosh,* from which is derived the word *midrash,* the method by which the sages culled their oral teachings from the Written Torah. For example, the Written Torah says, "You shall do no work on the Sabbath" (Exodus 20:10). But just what is it that constitutes "work"? The Torah is silent on this, but the scribes were not. Deciding that "work" refers to the types of activities used in the building of the sanctuary, the sages prohibited thirty-nine categories of labor: sowing, plowing, reaping, binding sheaves, threshing, winnowing, selecting, grinding, sifting, kneading, baking, shearing wool, washing wool, dyeing wool, spinning, weaving, making two loops, weaving two threads, separating two threads, tying, untying, sewing two stitches, tearing, trapping, slaughtering, flaying, salting meat, curing hide, scraping hide, cutting up hide, writing two letters, erasing two letters, building, tearing a building down, extinguishing a fire, kindling a fire, hitting with a hammer, taking an object from the private domain to the public, or transporting an object in the public domain (*Mishnah Shabbat* 7:2).

The opponents of the Pharisees, the Sadducees, saw in this a needless complication. But the laity who sought to live out the Torah's commands found in the extrapolations of the Pharisees a much-needed guide. The Pharisees, however, were not content to expand the Written Law and began a process of inventing new law that came from them alone. To legitimize this audacious enterprise, they once again applied their midrashic talents and found in the Written Torah a second revelation, the Oral Torah that is theirs alone: "Y-H-V-H said to Moses, 'Come up to Me to the mountain, and I will give you the stone tablets and the Torah and the Commandment which I have inscribed to instruct them'" (Exodus 24:12). While the Bible itself is clear that the tablets contained the Torah and the Commandment, in the hands of the scribes this passage came to affirm the existence of three gifts from God: the stone tablets refer to the Ten Commandments, the Torah to the Five Books of Moses, and the Commandment to the Mishnah, the Oral Law of the sages, finally committed to writing around 200CE. In one wave of the midrashic wand, the Pharisees doubled the revelation on Sinai.

The Sadducees, having only the Written Law without its midrashic revelations, were at a distinct disadvantage. They could not offer alternative Oral Law because they did not believe in a second oral revelation. All they could do was decry Pharisaic hubris. But again the Pharisees, unlike the aristocratic Sadducees, spoke for and to the people, and their new Torah was a welcome addition. So strong did the Oral Law become that the Pharisees could say of their work, "The pronouncements of the Scribes are far more precious than the words of the Bible" (Jerusalem Talmud, *Pe'ah* 2:6)!

# What Does Pirke Avot Mean?

When asking what *Pirke Avot* means, I am not asking what it says. You can read what it says, along with my commentary, later in this book. I am asking what does the very existence of *Pirke Avot* itself mean to Jews and to

Judaism? The answer is simple, startling, and still quite controversial.

The revelation that is *Pirke Avot* is rooted neither in sacrifice, prayer, nor halachic (legal) norms. It is rooted in study and ethical behavior. In this, *Pirke Avot* is closer to the Wisdom Literature of Proverbs than the legal literature of the Talmud. Indeed, I would argue that *Pirke Avot* is the last of the books of Jewish Wisdom, capping off a tradition that includes Proverbs, Job, Ecclesiastes, Sirach, Wisdom of Solomon, and (in my own understanding of Jesus as a Jewish wisdom sage) the Gospel According to Thomas. The concern in all these books is with understanding proverbs and parables in order to live the ethical principles at their root.

The meaning of *Pirke Avot* is that at the heart of Judaism is the desire to live out the core challenge of God to the Jewish people, and through them to all humanity: "Be holy as I, Y-H-V-H your God, am holy" (Leviticus 19:2).

What a strange command! We are to be holy as God is holy. We are to be, in a human way, what God is in a divine way. This single sentence erases any separation in essence between humanity and God.

Think of it this way: Imagine yourself saying to your dog, "Be human as I, your master, am human." Assume for a moment that your dog actually understood what you were saying. What must she be thinking? "This is madness. I'm a dog, not a human. We are different in kind, in essence. I cannot be as you are, for we are of different stuff." Your dog, no matter how she might desire otherwise, will not be able to live up to your challenge, and insisting that she do so is only going to highlight how different you are.

This is what Saint Paul argues when he says that the commandments of Judaism are not meant to save us but to show us how sinful we are: "No human being will be justified in His sight by works of the law, since through law comes knowledge of sin" (Romans 3:20). Because no one can live up to the challenge of the 613 commandments *(mitzvot)* imposed by the Rabbis, the only result of living under the law is to see how wicked you are. It is for this reason that God sends Jesus as Christ:

his death, the final cosmic sacrifice in the last years before the sacrificial cult falls before Rome, will do what all the millions of slaughtered animals could not do—get you right with God.

For Paul, the only alternative to animal sacrifice and living under the law is faith in the redemptive power of Jesus's death and resurrection. His logic is not faulty given his premise that you cannot be holy as God is holy. But what if he is wrong?

God's challenge to be holy makes sense if, unlike you and your dog, you and God share a common essence. I believe you do. As a wave is to the ocean, so you are to God. Just as the wave is the ocean extended in its time and place, so you are God manifest in your time and place. You are not other than God, though neither are you all of God. This is what I believe the prophet Isaiah means when he says, "The whole earth is full of God's glory" (Isaiah 6:3). Creation is not *for* the glory of God, it *is* the glory of God. Your task in this world is not to praise God but to be like God. But how?

That is where *Pirke Avot* comes in. While clearly a Jewish teaching addressed to Jewish people, *Pirke Avot*, like all great books of wisdom, speaks to all humanity. *Pirke Avot* teaches us how to be holy through the sayings of the rabbinic sages. For me, this is the lasting power of this book. Hence the "you" addressed by the sages is, in this translation, to be understood as referring to all humanity, especially you, the reader of this book.

Given this understanding of *Pirke Avot,* the commentary that accompanies my translation is concerned less with explicating the philosophy of the ancient Rabbis and more with uncovering the way to be holy. If you want to know more about the early Rabbis read any of the fine books listed in the Suggested Reading section at the back of this book. If you want to know more about how you can take up God's challenge to be holy, I suggest you turn the page now.

# Acknowledgments

My editor in this and many other books is Emily Wichland. We have never met, and I have no idea what she looks like. I know her voice from our phone conversations on my writing and her suggestions as to how to improve it, but I would not recognize it in any other context. Yet it is to this disembodied angel that I owe much of the quality of this book. She has a keen eye for error, and a strong nose for nonsense, and I rely on her to weed out both from my writing. If you find either, however, blame it on my insistence rather than her weakness. Emily, thanks again for midwifing this book.

# A Word on Translation

Every act of translation is an act of interpretation. Language is too rich, too nuanced, too alive, to lend itself to literalism. The translated text reflects the mind of its translator as well as the mind of its author. Regarding this translation of *Pirke Avot,* the mind of the translator is made plain in the commentary that accompanies the text. Yet there are two words in particular that require a bit more explanation: *Adonai,* "God," and *Olam HaBa,* "the World to Come."

God is not the focus of *Pirke Avot.* God neither acts nor speaks in this collection of rabbinic proverbs, yet the Name of God appears quite frequently and must be dealt with honestly. In most translations, the four-letter Name of God, the Tetragrammaton (four-lettered), Y-H-V-H, is translated in most texts as "Lord." This comes from the third-century-BCE Jewish practice of reading *Adonai*/Lord whenever the Tetragrammaton appears in a text so as not to violate the law against pronouncing God's Name (Exodus 20:7; Deuteronomy 5:11). In the Middle Ages, Christian scholars who read the Bible in its original Hebrew blended the vowels of *Adonai* with the four consonants Y-H-V-H to create the word "Jehovah."

Despite its pedigree, however, *Adonai*/Lord distorts the very essence of Y-H-V-H. God's Name, referred to as *HaShem*/the Name by traditional Jews, is a variation of the Hebrew verb "to be." It is free from both the gender and political biases that "Lord" carries with it. In addition, calling God "Lord" implies that God is a being, albeit the Supreme Being. But Y-H-V-H refers not to *a* being, but to *being* itself. God is what is, and was and will be. Hence God self-identifies to Moses at the Burning Bush as *Ehyeh asher Ehyeh,* "I will be what I will be" (Exodus 3:14).

God will be what God will be. God is not static. God doesn't change; God *is* change. God is reality and reality is in constant creative flux. God, as the Hebrew makes clear, is not a noun but a verb. And what does this Verb do? It creates and reveals itself to, with, in, and through its creation. God is all that is. God is you, all of you, for if God were less than you, God would be limited, and a limited god is not God.

The challenge is how to translate Y-H-V-H so as not to promote a static, male, patriarchal, hierarchical, and militaristic Lord. In an earlier poetic interpretation of *Pirke Avot (Wisdom of the Sages,* Bell Tower), I used the word "Reality" for Y-H-V-H. God is all that is, so God is reality. This is not bad, but for this more philosophical translation, it seems somehow insufficient. When translating selections of the Hebrew prophets (see *The Hebrew Prophets: Selections Annotated and Explained,* SkyLight Paths), I chose "the One Who Is." This, too, is both right and insufficient. If I could borrow a word from Sanskrit, I would translate Y-H-V-H as *tathata,* or "suchness." Or, if Chinese where available to me, I would use "Tao," recalling the opening line of the *Tao Te Ching,* "The tao that can be named is not the eternal Tao." But such borrowings would make matters worse. So I have decided simply to use the word "God," and rely on my commentary and this brief explanation to make it clear that I am referring not to a divine object but to the pure Subject of all reality: the I Am that you are.

The second challenge in *Pirke Avot* is the phrase *Olam HaBa,* "the World to Come." Judaism has no dogmatic position on the afterlife. The Hebrew Bible has little interest in the world to come. Genesis tells us that when people die they go to *sheol,* the grave (Genesis 37:35). *Sheol* may be more than a burial plot, however, and Saul's successful communication with Samuel after the latter's death suggests that something of the deceased survives death (1 Samuel 28). What that "more" is gives rise to speculation on the afterlife.

Ezekiel, for example, speaks of the resurrection of the "dry bones," which God says represent the entire Jewish people (Ezekiel 37:11). The Book of Daniel tells us that "many of those who sleep in the dusty earth will awaken: these for everlasting life and these for shame, for everlasting abhorrence" (Daniel 12:2).

Most scholars believe that the ideas expressed in Daniel, the expectation of judgment and eternal reward or punishment, came into Judaism through Persian and Greek influences picked up during the Babylonian exile (598–538BCE). The idea that God would mete out justice in an afterlife allowed the Jews to maintain their faith during times of injustice, especially during the persecution of the Jews by Antiochus that led to the Maccabean revolt (167–164BCE).

The term *Olam HaBa,* "the World to Come," juxtaposed with *olam hazeh,* "this world," comes from Hellenistic Jewish literature such as the *Apocalypse of Enoch* (71:15), written some time between 200BCE and 50CE. The notion of the soul's immortality comes into Judaism during this time as well, reflecting the influence of Greek and Roman philosophy. The Pharisees took the notion to heart and made it a central part of their Judaism, much to the dismay of their Saducean rivals, for whom such a notion was an alien intrusion. The Pharisees make their attachment to immortality powerfully clear in *Sanhedrin* 10:1, which is then repeated in the prologue to *Pirke Avot:* "All Israel has a place in the World to Come except those who say there is no World to Come."

Just what *Olam HaBa* is, however, is unclear. Having affirmed its existence, the Rabbis take little interest in its details. The third-century Rabbi Yochanan bar Nappaha speaks for mainstream rabbinic tradition when he says, "All the prophets prophesied only about the days of the Messiah, but of the World to Come, 'the eye has not seen it, O God' (Isaiah 64:3)" (*Sanhedrin* 99a; *Berachot* 34b).

If no eye has seen it, how are we to understand it? In my translation of *Pirke Avot* I have chosen to translate the phrase literally as "the World to Come," allowing my commentary to articulate what the phrase means in context. It may help, however, to know from the start just what my own understanding of *Olam HaBa* really is.

I take my understanding from Martin Buber's masterful *The Way of Man According to the Teaching of Hasidism* (Secaucus, NJ: Citadel Press,

1966).Buber writes, "It is said of a certain Talmudic master that the paths of heaven were as bright to him as the streets of his native town. Hasidism inverts the order: It is a greater thing if the streets of your native town are as bright to you as the paths of heaven. For it is here, where we stand, that we should try to make shine the light of the hidden divine life" (p.38).

*Olam HaBa,* here equated with heaven, is not an alternative to *olam hazeh,* but rather a way of being in *olam hazeh* that sees it as the hidden life of God. *Olam HaBa* is a state of mind, what the Hasidim call *mochin d'gadlut,* "spacious mind." Spacious mind sees this world as the hidden life of God. The mind that fails to see this world as divine, and which imagines *Olam HaBa* as other than *olam hazeh,* is *mochin d'katnut,* "narrow mind."

Both minds exist in you. Narrow mind is the mind that focuses on the seeming duality of things: I and Thou, us and them, up and down, in and out, good and evil. Spacious mind is the mind that sees duality in the larger frame of nonduality. Spacious mind is the mind that understands God when God says, "I form light and create darkness, I make goodness and create evil, I, Y-H-V-H, do all these things" (Isaiah 45:7). Narrow mind sees the world as us and them, good and evil, and desires a world to come that is us without them, and good without evil. Spacious mind knows this desire to be as ridiculous as to desire a world of up without down, or in without out. To narrow mind everything is other; to spacious mind everything is one.

*Olam HaBa* is *olam hazeh* when seen from spacious mind. Yet *Olam HaBa* is more than a psychological shift of awareness; it also carries with it a political transformation.

When you realize God is all, you engage all as God. You meet each being as a manifestation of the One Being and treat all things with justice, compassion, and humility. This is the politics of *Olam HaBa* that *Pirke Avot* promotes.

Living the awakened life of *mochin d'gadlut,* both psychologically and politically, is what *Pirke Avot* is all about. I hope that my translation helps you in both regards.

# Biographical Sketches of the Rabbis in Pirke Avot

## Abba Shaul

Abba Shaul is little remembered in the Talmud. Some say he was a gravedigger, while others say he was baker in the employ of Yehudah HaNasi (*Pesach* 34a; *Niddah* 24b).

## Akavia ben Mahalalel

Akavia ben Mahalalel was called "rebellious" but was not excommunicated because his decisions were rooted in tradition (*Sanhedrin* 88a). He disagreed with his colleagues on four issues, and while insisting he was wrong, the sages offered him the position of *Av Bet Din* if he would change his mind and side with the majority. Akavia refused, saying, "Let it not be said that because of prestige Akavia retreated!" (*Mishnah Eduyot* 5:6).

# Akiva

Akiva, born around the year 20CE, was said to have lived 120 years (*Sifrei Berachah* 36). He spent the first forty years of his life as an illiterate shepherd in the employ of Kalba Savuah, one of Jerusalem's wealthiest men. Savuah's daughter Rachel fell in love with Akiva and promised to marry him if he would learn Torah. He agreed, but when Savuah discovered this, he banished both Akiva and his daughter from his home. The two lived in abject poverty. When Akiva became a renowned scholar, Savuah realized his mistake and supported them. Akiva was a great *Merkava* mystic, engaging in the mysticism that flourished in Palestine during the first century CE, but moved its center to Babylonia from the seventh to the eleventh century. He was said to be among the four sages who entered heaven through mystic means and was the only of the four to survive the experience intact. Akiva declared Bar Kochba to be the Messiah and supported his rebellion against Rome (132–135CE). After the fall of Beitar and the death of Bar Kochba, Akiva was captured and sentenced to be flayed alive with iron combs. He died reciting the *Sh'ma* ("Hear, O Israel, Y-H-V-H is our God, Y-H-V-H is One") in the presence of his disciples.

## Antigonus

Antigonus of Socho was a second-century-BCE sage. Rabbinic tradition holds that Antigonus's teaching that you should not serve God in hopes of a reward was misunderstood by two of his students to mean that there is no life after death. One of these, Tzadok, is said to have founded the Sadducees, a sect of Judaism that denied an afterlife.

## Avtalyon

Avtalyon was *Av Bet Din* in Shemayah's Sanhedrin, and both of them were converts to Judaism, said to be descendants of the Assyrian king Sancherev (*Gittin* 57b).

## Ben Azzai

Ben Azzai, a colleague of Ben Zoma's in both scholarship and mysticism, was betrothed to Rabbi Akiva's daughter Rachel but never married her, preferring to devote himself exclusively to study. Entering heaven with Akiva, Zoma, and Ben Avuya, it is said that as soon as he "caught a glimpse" of heaven he died. "Of him Scripture says: Precious in the eyes of Y-H-V-H is the death of God's saints (Psalm 116:15)" (*Chagigah* 14b).

## Ben Bag Bag

Ben Bag Bag was a convert to Judaism (*Tosefta Chagigah* 9b), and some say he was the gentile who demanded that Hillel teach him the entire Torah while standing on one foot. Bag Bag was not his real name, but a short form of *ben ger ben giyoret* (son of male and female converts). The name was given to him to protect his true identity from the Romans, who had decreed that conversion to Judaism was a capital offense.

## Ben Hei Hei

Ben Hei Hei, like Ben Bag Bag, was a convert to Judaism (*Tosefta Chagigah* 9b) at a time when the Romans had made conversion to Judaism punishable by death. *Hei* is the fifth letter of the Hebrew alphabet and the letter added to the names of Abram and Sarai in Genesis when they made their covenant with God. Abram becomes Abra*H*am and Sarai becomes Sara *H* (Genesis 17:5, 17:15). Since all converts to Judaism are considered in the lineage of Abraham and Sarah and are called *ben* or *bat Avraham v'Sarah* (son or daughter of Abraham and Sarah), the double *hei* was used to identify Ben Hei Hei as a Jew and yet conceal his true identity from the Romans.

## Ben Zoma

Ben Zoma, one of the wisest men of his time, was a mystic steeped in the secrets of the *Merkava* (Chariot). He was one of the four mystic sages who, using contemplative practices, "entered the Garden" (heaven). "Four men entered the Garden—Ben Azzai, Ben Zoma, Acher [Elisha ben Avuya], and Rabbi Akiva.... Ben Zoma looked and lost his mind. Of him Scripture says: If you find honey, eat only a moderate amount, lest you become sick from overindulging (Proverbs 25:16)" (*Chagigah* 14b).

## Chalafta ben Dosa

Chalafta ben Dosa of Kfar Chanania lived during the second half of the second century CE.

## Chanania ben Akashia

Chanania ben Akashia has only one halachic ruling preserved in his name (*Tosefta Shekalim* 3:18). His teaching that Torah and *mitzvot* (commandments) were given to the Jews in order to confer merit upon them traditionally concludes each chapter of *Pirke Avot*. We have used it here to conclude the entire book.

# Rabbi Chanina ben Chachinai

Rabbi Chanina ben Chachinai was one of the Ten Martyrs *(Aseret Harugei Melachot)* killed by the Romans during the period of the destruction of the Second Temple (70CE). While the Ten Martyrs were not killed at the same time, their names are listed together and recited as part of the Tisha b'Av and Yom Kippur liturgies. In addition to Rabbi Chanina ben Chachinai, the other martyred rabbis were Rabban Shimon Ben Gamliel, Rabbi Yishmael ben Elisha, Rabbi Akiva, Rabbi Chanina ben Tradyon, Rabbi Chutzpis, Rabbi Elazar ben Shamua, Rabbi Yesheivav, Rabbi Elazar ben Damah, and Rabbi Yehudah ben Bava.

# Chanina ben Dosa

Chanina ben Dosa lived near the close of the Second Temple period (the Temple was destroyed in 70CE) and was considered one of the most righteous men of his time. Scrupulous in his observance of the law, Chanina was known for starting the Sabbath Friday afternoon rather than Friday evening (*Bereshit Rabbah* 10:8).

## Chanina ben Tradyon

Chanina ben Tradyon was one of the Ten Martyrs executed during the Roman persecution following the Bar Kochba revolt (132–135CE). The charge against him was teaching Torah and convening public gatherings, both of which were outlawed by Rome. He was wrapped in the Torah scroll from which he had been teaching and burned at the stake. As he was dying, his students asked him what he saw. He replied that as the Torah parchment was consumed, the letters left the scroll and soared to heaven. Chanina's wife was also executed and his daughter sold into prostitution, from which she was rescued by her sister, Beruriah, and her brother-in-law, Rabbi Meir.

## Dosa ben Harkinas

Dosa ben Harkinas was a wealthy first-generation sage. He is noted for being in conflict with the majority of sages over issues surrounding cleanliness and contact with a human corpse. Dosa ben Harkinas tended to be less stringent than the majority in these matters (*Mishnah Eduyot* 3:1).

## Dostai bar Yannai

Dostai bar Yannai was known as a *baal aggadah,* a master of stories. *Aggadot* (stories) explore ethical ideas, biblical characters, or narrative moments in the Torah.

## Elazar of Bartosa

Elazar of Bartosa was famous for his generosity. Once, when going to purchase his daughter's trousseau, he noticed that the charity collectors were avoiding him for fear of bankrupting him. Discovering that they were raising money to cover the wedding of two orphans, he gave them all of his own money but one small coin. He used that coin to buy a bit of grain that he stored in the granary. There it multiplied until it filled the entire granary. He then distributed the grain to the poor (*Taanit* 3:7).

## Elazar ben Arach

Elazar ben Arach was capable of great mystic feats based on his studies of the *Merkava.* Once while walking with his teacher, Yochanan ben Zakkai, he expounded on the mystery of the Divine Chariot. So powerful was his teaching that fire descended from heaven, igniting the trees all around, which then began to sing. When Ben Zakkai died, Elazar did not retire to Yavneh, the center for Jewish learning, but, following his wife's advice, moved to a wealthy community in Emmanus, where he slowly forgot all his learning. Elijah the Prophet is said to have visited him and retaught him all he had forgotten.

## Elazar ben Azariah

Elazar ben Azariah was a Torah prodigy who, at the age of eighteen, was asked to replace Rabban Gamliel, who had been deposed as *Nasi* and sent into exile. He consulted with his wife and, with her support, took the position. Elazar was prematurely gray, giving him the look of an elder, and extremely wealthy. When Rabban Gamliel was reinstated as *Nasi,* he asked that Elazar become *Av Bet Din* and teach one out of every three or four Sabbaths (Jerusalem Talmud, *Berachot* 4:1; *Berachot* 27b–28a).

## Elazar ben Shamua

Elazar ben Shamua was one of the last disciples of Rabbi Akiva. When the Romans made ordination a capital crime, Elazar and four other students of Akiva were ordained by Rabbi Yehudah ben Bava, who was executed for doing so. Elazar and the others escaped. Elazar was martyred at the age of 105.

## Elazar HaKappar

Elazar HaKappar was a member of the court of Yehudah HaNasi. In seeking to understand the sin of a Nazirite (a person who devotes him-or herself to God by refusing, among other things, to drink wine), mentioned in Numbers (6:11), Elazar argued that it was the refusal to drink wine that was the sin. From this he argued that pleasure was a gift from God and that by denying oneself life's enjoyments one sins against God (*Taanit* 11a).

## Elazar the Moda'ite

Elazar the Moda'ite was a noted aggadist (one who invents tales based on the Bible and illustrating biblical principles) and uncle to Bar Kochba, who led the Jewish rebellion against Rome (132–135CE). Unjustly suspected of collaborating with Rome during the three-year siege of Beitar, Elazar was slain by his nephew. The death of Elazar was said to be the cause of Bar Kochba's defeat (Jerusalem Talmud, *Taanit* 4:5).

## Eliezer ben Chisma

Eliezer ben Chisma was a poor scholar known for his great physical strength. "Chisma" (strong) was probably not his father's name, but a nickname bestowed upon him. Rabban Gamliel gave Eliezer a job at the academy in Yavneh to help him earn a living and continue his studies.

## Eliezer ben Hyrkanos

Eliezer ben Hyrkanos worked unhappily tending his wealthy father's estates. At the age of twenty-eight he asked permission from his father to leave and study Torah. His father scornfully refused to let him go. Elijah the Prophet is said to have visited Eliezer, urging him to study in Jerusalem. He ran away to study and was so poor that he was forced to eat dirt in order not to starve. When his teachers discovered this, they secured him a stipend so he could continue his studies. During Vespasian's siege of Jerusalem, Eliezer aided his teacher, Yochanan ben Zakkai, in his escape from the city to meet with Vespasian (*Gittin* 56a). In a legal dispute with the other sages, Eliezer called on God to affirm the correctness of his ruling. God did, but the sages rejected this and excommunicated Eliezer.

## Eliezer ben Yaakov

Eliezer ben Yaakov was a student of Rabbi Akiva's who would often debate the law with Rabbi Meir (*Rosh HaShanah* 4b).

# Elisha ben Avuya

Elisha ben Avuya was one of the four rabbis who, using the mystic tools of the *Merkava* (Chariot mysticism), experienced heaven while yet alive. Although he was called Acher (the Other) because the experience robbed him of his faith and he was shunned by many sages, his wisdom was still prized, and he continued to teach Torah to his disciple Rabbi Meir. Other sages say he lost his faith because of the injustices suffered by the Jews of his day (Jerusalem Talmud, *Chagigah* 2:1). Elisha ben Avuya is the protagonist in Milton Steinberg's excellent novel *As a Driven Leaf*.

# Gamliel

Gamliel, son of Shimon ben Gamliel, was the *Nasi* of the academy at Yavneh, the center for Jewish learning established after the fall of the Second Temple to Rome in 70CE. Gamliel, who was the first sage to hold the title *rabban,* "teacher," sought to unify all halachic (legal) rulings in accordance with the standards set by the school of Hillel. It was under Gamliel that the prayer services of the Jews were first formalized. He established the *Shemoneh Esrei* (Eighteen Benedictions) as obligatory and unchangeable. Rabbis Akiva and Yehoshua disagreed and allowed a shorter version of the prayer, and Rabbi Eliezer argued that fixed prayer is ineffective (*Mishnah Berachot* 4:5).

# Gamliel ben Yehudah HaNasi

Gamliel ben Yehudah HaNasi succeeded his father, Yehudah HaNasi, as *Nasi,* having been chosen by his father on the latter's deathbed.

# Hillel

Hillel was one of the greatest sages of the Sanhedrin. An exceedingly poor man, Hillel worked as a day laborer. Each day he earned enough to pay his family's expenses and to bribe a guard at the academy to let him in to listen to the deliberations of the sages. One day he failed to earn enough to bribe the guard. He climbed up onto the roof of the academy and listened in through the skylight. It began to snow, and Hillel succumbed to the cold and fell asleep. In the morning Avtalyon and Shemayah found him on the roof buried in snow. They brought him inside and, despite it being the Sabbath, cleaned him, anointed him with oil, and warmed him by the fire saying, "For this cause it is worth desecrating the Sabbath" (*Yoma* 35b). Hillel is known for his humility and love for all people.

## Levitas of Yavneh

Levitas of Yavneh, a third-generation sage, appears only once in the Talmud.

## Matya ben Charash

Matya ben Charash escaped the persecution of the Jews after the failure of Bar Kochba and set up an academy in Rome. Satan was jealous of Matya's piety and sought to trick him into sinning by disguising himself as a beautiful woman and luring Matya from his prayers. Matya could not avoid the woman's stares, so he took a nail and blinded himself. Satan was overcome by this act of devotion, and God sent the angel Raphael to heal Matya. Matya refused, and God took responsibility for what Satan had done and healed Matya directly.

# Meir

Meir was a descendant of converts to Judaism, and husband of the famous wise woman Beruriah. Meir, which means "the illuminator," was probably an honorific title bestowed by colleagues, who said of him, "He enlightened the eyes of the scholars" (*Eruvin* 13b). Meir's mind was considered incredibly sharp. "It is as if he is uprooting two mountains and grinding them against one another" (*Sanhedrin* 24a). He enlivened his lectures with fables, and was said to have memorized three hundred fox tales (*Sanhedrin* 38b).

## Nechunya ben Hakanah

Nechunya ben Hakanah was known for his long life, which he attributed to his good relationships with his colleagues and his willingness to forgive all offenses each evening before going to sleep.

## Nehorai

Nehorai lived in the second century CE. In contrast to the majority of sages who sought to integrate labor with study, teaching that a father was obligated to teach his son a trade, Nehorai taught that he would teach his son only Torah, for it is Torah alone that will earn him a place in the World to Come.

## Nittai of Arbel

Nittai of Arbel was *Av Bet Din* in Yehoshua ben Perachyah's Sanhedrin.

## Shammai

Shammai, who made his living as a contractor and builder, is best known as the *Av Bet Din* during Hillel's term as *Nasi*. A strict interpreter of the law, Shammai and Hillel and their respective schools disagreed over hundreds of rulings. For over three years the schools of Shammai and Hillel argued. At last a heavenly voice said, "Both are the words of the living God, but the law is in agreement with Hillel." The ruling went to the school of Hillel because they were kind, modest, and open to considering the position of Shammai, while the school of Shammai listened only to themselves (*Eruvin* 13b). Perhaps the best-known story of Shammai is that of the gentile who came to him on a construction site and demanded Shammai teach him the entire Torah while standing on one foot. Shammai chased the man away with a level. The gentile then went to Hillel with the same request. Hillel complied saying, "That which is hurtful to you, do not do to others. That is the whole of the law. All the rest is commentary. Now go and study it" (*Shabbat* 31a).

# Shemayah

Shemayah became *Nasi* in 65BCE. He believed strongly in the dignity of manual labor and encouraged his fellow sages to work as well as study.

# Shimon ben Yochai

Often known as Shimon bar Yochai but correctly translated from Hebrew as Shimon ben Yochai, he was hunted by the Romans for preaching against the state. He and his son, Rabbi Elazar, hid for twelve years in a cave and studied Torah. Elijah the Prophet was sent by God to tell them it was safe to return home, but when they emerged from the cave and saw people engaged in temporal labor, fire escaped from their eyes and set things ablaze. God ordered them back into the cave for another year to learn how to adapt to the everyday world. Shimon ben Yochai is said to be the author of the *Zohar*, the central text of Kabbalah.

## Shimon ben Elazar

Shimon ben Elazar is noted for preserving a tradition established by Ezra, who taught that we should read the curses associated with breaking God's covenant with the Hebrews (Leviticus 26:14ff) before the holy day of Shavuot (commemorating the giving of the Ten Commandments on Mount Sinai), and the curses (Deuteronomy 28:15ff) before the holy day of Rosh HaShanah (the Jewish New Year).

## Shimon ben Gamliel

Shimon ben Gamliel, grandson of Hillel and father of Rabban Gamliel, was beheaded by the Romans in 50CE.

## Shimon ben Menasya

Shimon ben Menasya was a colleague of Yehudah HaNasi. He was known for dividing his day into three parts: one-third in study, one-third in prayer, and one-third in labor.

## Shimon ben Netanel

Shimon ben Netanel, along with Yose HaKohen, was a student of *Merkava* mysticism, in which he was called "well versed" (Jerusalem Talmud, *Chagigah* 2:1).

## Shimon ben Shatach

Shimon ben Shatach, the first Pharisee to join the Sanhedrin, was instrumental in shifting control of the Sanhedrin from the Sadducees to Pharisees. He insisted that all rulings of the Sanhedrin be rooted in proofs derived from the Torah. Since the Sadducees lacked the interpretive skills honed by the Pharisees, the latter began to replace the former in the Sanhedrin.

## Shimon ben Yehudah

Shimon ben Yehudah transmitted teachings in the name of his rabbi, Shimon ben Yochai.

# Shimon HaTzadik

Shimon HaTzadik (Simon the Righteous) was the High Priest *(Kohen Gadol)* in the early second century BCE. Playing a bridge role between the prophetic and rabbinic periods of Jewish history, he was one of the sages who set the biblical canon and is the earliest authority named in *Pirke Avot*.

# Shmuel HaKattan

Shmuel HaKattan was called *HaKattan* (the Small) due to his modesty, not his size. He composed *Birkat HaMinim* (the Blessing against Heretics), which was included in the *Shemoneh Esrei,* the Eighteen Benedictions (bringing the total to nineteen) that are the central prayers of every service.

# Tarfon

Tarfon was a leader in the city of Lod (*Mishnah Bava Metzia* 4:3) who moved to Yavneh during Rabban Gamliel's time as *Nasi*. Rabbi Tarfon perfected a Socratic teaching style, asking his students questions and inviting discussion. He would often engage his students in dialogue opening with "Shall I ask?" (*Tosefta Berachot* 4:16). He was famous for his love of his family and devotion to his mother. Once, when his mother was walking in the yard on Shabbat, her shoe broke. Rabbi Tarfon crawled before her, allowing her to place her feet on his hands so as to avoid walking in the dirt (Jerusalem Talmud, *Kedushin* 1:7).

# Tzadok

Tzadok was a student of the school of Shammai who often ruled in accordance with the competing school of Hillel. Tzadok lived through the destruction of the Second Temple in 70CE, serving as a rabbinic judge in Yavneh.

# Yaakov

Yaakov was a teacher in the yeshiva (academy) of Rabban Shimon ben Gamliel. He uncovered a plot to depose Shimon by publicly quizzing him on tractate *Uktzin* with which the rabbi was unfamiliar. Yaakov stood near Rabban Shimon and began to study the tractate aloud. Eventually Rabban Shimon caught on and studied the tractate himself, thus passing the challenge and retaining his post.

## Yannai

Yannai was a fourth-or fifth-generation sage who taught in the name of Rabban Shimon ben Gamliel.

## Yehoshua ben Chanania

Yehoshua ben Chanania was a poor blacksmith (*Berachot* 28a) and needle maker (*Berachot* 4:1) of the tribe of Levi, who sang in the Temple (*Arachin* 11b). He was fluent in several languages, including Greek, and had knowledge of mathematics and astronomy. While the chief opponent of Rabbi Eliezer ben Hyrkanos and complicit in his excommunication, he defended the rabbi's teachings after his death and refused to allow them to be refuted by other sages. It was Yehoshua who insisted the World to Come was not exclusive to Jews and that the righteous of all peoples have a place in heaven.

## Yehoshua ben Levi

Yehoshua ben Levi was called a master of the Mishnah and was responsible for instituting the custom of reciting the *Sh'ma* ("Hear, O Israel, Y-H-V-H is our God, Y-H-V-H is One") at bedtime. His son, Rabbi Yosef, fell ill and had a near-death experience. Yehoshua asked him what he saw in heaven, and his son said, "I saw a world upside down: the powerful in this world were the least in the next, and the least in this world were the powerful in the next." Yehoshua replied, "My son, you have seen the world clearly" (*Pesach* 50a).

## Yehoshua ben Perachyah

Yehoshua ben Perachyah served as *Nasi* of the Sanhedrin during the Hasmonean rule. The Hasmonean king Alexander Yanni (103–76BCE) sought to crush the Sanhedrin and executed eight hundred sages. Yehoshua ben Perachyah fled to Alexandria, Egypt. According to

Jewish tradition (*Sotah* 47a), Yehoshua was accompanied by Jesus, who returned with him to Jerusalem once the danger had passed.

## Yehudah ben Tabbai

Yehudah ben Tabbai served with Shimon ben Shatach as leaders of the Sanhedrin. There is some confusion as to who was *Nasi* and who was *Av Bet Din*. Perhaps both are true. During the Hasmonean persecutions, Shimon ben Shatach was appointed *Nasi,* and Yehudah ben Tabbai was *Av Bet Din*. Shimon was forced to flee and was thought dead. Yehudah became *Nasi* in his stead, but when Shimon returned, he reclaimed his position as *Nasi,* and Yehudah once again became *Av Bet Din* (Jerusalem Talmud, *Chagigah* 2:2; *Sanhedrin* 6:9).

## Yehudah ben Tema

Yehudah ben Tema taught sometime after the destruction of the Second Temple (70CE).

## Yehudah HaNasi

Yehudah HaNasi (Judah the Prince) was the oldest son of Rabban Gamliel. Born during the Hadrianic persecutions, when circumcision was outlawed, Yehudah was secretly circumcised. Word got out, and his mother was ordered to bring him to the emperor to be killed. On the journey, a Roman woman gave birth and offered to temporarily switch babies with Yehudah's mother so that the emperor would think the rumors of his circumcision were false and thus spare his life. Seeing that the Roman Empire was growing and that Jews were scattering throughout the empire, Yehudah HaNasi ordered that the Oral Law be written down to protect it from being forgotten or misquoted. This text is called the Mishnah.

## Yishmael

Yishmael was a master midrashist (inventing new narratives to interpret the law). A young child during the time of the destruction of the Second Temple in 70CE, Yishmael was imprisoned in

Rome and was ransomed by Rabbi Yehoshua, who recognized in him the potential to be a great scholar.

## Yishmael bar Rabbi Yose

Yishmael bar Rabbi Yose, a fifth-generation sage, earned his living selling clothing (*Bava Metzia* 73). A judge in Yehudah HaNasi's court, he was known for his impartiality.

## Yochanan ben Beroka

Yochanan ben Beroka, a third-generation sage and friend of Eliezer ben Chisma, also suffered from poverty and benefited with his friend from Rabban Gamliel's offer of work in Yavneh.

## Yochanan ben Zakkai

Yochanan ben Zakkai, a student of Hillel's, is thought to have lived 120 years. The first forty he spent in business, the second forty in study, and the third forty he devoted to teaching. It is possible that he was the *Av Bet Din* during the time that Rabban Shimon ben Gamliel was *Nasi.* Yochanan ben Zakkai lived in Jerusalem during the three-year siege by the Roman general Vespasian. The city was under the grip of fanatics who wanted to battle Rome. Yochanan wanted to sue for peace. To meet with Vespasian, he faked his own death and was carried out of the city in a coffin, according to the law that no one be buried within the city walls. Once outside the city, he met with Vespasian, prophesying that the general would soon be emperor of Rome and asking him to spare the sages and allow them to establish an academy in the city of Yavneh (*Gittin* 56b). The academy ensured the survival of Judaism.

# Yochanan the Sandal Maker

Yochanan the Sandal Maker served as a go-between, linking the sages with Akiva when Akiva was imprisoned following the collapse of the Bar Kochba revolt. Yochanan would pace back and forth beneath the window to Akiva's cell pretending to sell his wares. As he called out to potential customers, he would slip in questions of law addressed to Rabbi Akiva. Akiva would yell back as if he were a customer and weave his ruling into his shopping inquiries.

## Yonatan

Yonatan was a member of the priestly class. It was Yonatan who ruled that saving a life supersedes observing the Sabbath, arguing that "the Sabbath is given to you; you are not given to the Sabbath" (*Yoma* 85b).

## Yose bar Yehudah

Yose bar Yehudah of Kfar HaBavli is mentioned only once in the entire Talmud (*Pirke Avot* 5:20), and nothing is known of him other than that.

## Yose ben Kisma

Yose ben Kisma lived during the time of the Bar Kochba revolt and urged people to submit to the laws of Rome rather than die resisting them.

## Yose ben Yochanan

Yose ben Yochanan of Jerusalem was *Av Bet Din* of Yose ben Yoezer's Sanhedrin. The *Av Bet Din* presided over the Sanhedrin in the absence of the *Nasi* and was the chief of the Sanhedrin when it sat to hear criminal cases.

## Yose ben Yoezer

Yose ben Yoezer Tz'redah came from a priestly family and was the first to lead the Sanhedrin as *Nasi.* Yose ben Yoezer was renowned for his piety and learning. His fellow sages called him "the pious one of the priesthood" (*Mishnah Chagigah* 2:7).

## Yose HaKohen

Yose HaKohen lived at the end of the first century CE. A student of *Merkava* mysticism under Rabbi Yehoshua ben Chanania, he engaged in a variety of austere practices to induce visions of the Divine Chariot described by the prophet Ezekiel (Ezekiel 1).

# Ethics of the Sages

## Prologue1

All Israel[2] partakes in the World to Come,[3]
as it is said,
"And your people are all righteous;
they shall inherit the land forever;
they are the branch,[4] I am the Tree,
My handiwork,[5] in which to take pride."[6]

**1** The Prologue is appended to *Pirke Avot* from another Talmudic text, *Sanhedrin* 90a.

**2** Israel is the Torah's archetype of the spiritually realized human being, the wounded warrior (Genesis 32:26) who "wrestles with the Divine" (Genesis 32:29) and "walks at the pace of the nursing cows and children" (Genesis 33:14). Anyone who carries (rather than projects) her own shadow, who reveals the holy manifest as the ordinary, and who seeks justice for the powerless is Israel.

**3** The World to Come, what Jesus calls the Kingdom of God, is "not in heaven," but "in your heart" (Deuteronomy 30:14); not outside of you, but within you (Luke 17:21). The World to Come is this world seen without the delusions of *mochin d'katnut,* "narrow mind," and the fear, violence, and greed that arise from them.

**4** You are an extension of God as a branch is an extension of a tree. You are the way God manifests in your place and time. When you realize this, you see the world through *mochin d'gadlut,* "spacious mind"; love replaces fear, and justice, compassion, and humility (Micah 6:8) transform the land and all who inherit it.

**5** You are God's handiwork, the way God does what it is you are called to do.

**6** Isaiah 60:21.

# Chapter One

1:1
Moses received Torah[1] from Sinai[2]
and transmitted[3] it to Joshua;
Joshua transmitted it to the elders;
the elders to the prophets;
and the prophets to the sages of the
 Great Assembly[4]
who taught three things:
Be careful in judgment;[5]
raise up many disciples;[6]
and surround Torah with a hedge.[7]

1:2
Shimon HaTzadik was among the last
 of the Great Assembly.
He used to say,
The world rests on three things:
on wisdom,
on surrender,
on compassion.[8]

1:3
Antigonus of Socho received
 transmission from Shimon HaTzadik.
He used to say,

Do not serve in order to earn reward;
serve only to serve.
In this way the awe of heaven will be
 upon you.[9]

## 1:4
Yose ben Yoezer Tz'redah and Yose ben
 Yochanan of Jerusalem
received transmission from Antigonus
 and Shimon.

Yose ben Yoezer teaches,
Make your home a meeting place for
 the wise;[10]
sit in the dust of their feet;[11]
and drink in their wisdom thirstily.[12]

## 1:5
Open your house to everyone;
treat the poor as family;[13]
and do not disrespect women with idle
 chatter.
This is true not only regarding a wife,
 but all women,
for anyone who seeks to impress
 women with idle chatter
attracts evil, forgets wisdom, and
 inherits hell.[14]

1:6
Yehoshua ben Perachyah and Nittai of Arbel
received transmission from Yose ben Yoezer and Yose ben Yochanan.

Yehoshua ben Perachyah teaches,
Make yourself worthy of a teacher,[15]
secure for yourself a friend,[16]
and judge everyone favorably.[17]

1:7
Nittai of Arbel teaches,
Distance yourself from a bad neighbor,[18]
do not collaborate with evil,[19]
and do not despair of justice.[20]

1:8
Yehudah ben Tabbai and Shimon ben Shatach
received transmission from Yehoshua ben Perachyah and Nittai of Arbel.

Yehudah ben Tabbai teaches,
When called to judge, do not act as a lawyer;
when listening to litigants, consider them both capable of guilt;

when judgment is accepted, consider them both innocent.[21]

1:9
Shimon ben Shatach teaches,
Question matters deeply;
and be careful with your phrasing
lest you reveal your bias
and hear only what you want to hear
rather than what is true.[22]

1:10
Shemayah and Avtalyon received
 transmission from
Yehudah ben Tabbai and Shimon ben
 Shatach.
Shemayah teaches,
Love work,[23]
shun clerics,
and do not get cozy with the
 government.[24]

1:11
Avtalyon teaches,
Do not mistake words for truth
lest you become exiled in cleverness
where every well is poison,
and all who drink from them will die,[25]

and thus diminish the Name of Heaven.[26]

1:12
Hillel and Shammai received transmission from Shemayah and Avtalyon.
Hillel teaches,
Discipline yourself in the way of Aaron,[27] loving peace and pursuing peace;[28] loving people and bringing them to Torah.[29]

1:13
Hillel used to teach,
Seek after fame, and you will lose honor;[30]
Cling to knowledge, and you will forget wisdom;[31]
Cease to learn, and you cease to live;[32]
Exploit what you know, and wisdom will evade you.[33]

1:14
Hillel teaches,
If I am not for myself, who will be for me?[34]

But if I am only for myself, what am I?[35]
And if not now, when?[36]

1:15
Shammai teaches,
Discipline yourself to study wisdom:
say little and do much;
welcome everyone with grace.[37]

1:16
Rabban Gamliel used to say,
Get for yourself a teacher.
Free yourself from doubt.
Do not guess when tithing.[38]

1:17
Shimon ben Gamliel teaches,
I was raised on the talk of sages,
and yet I find nothing more true than silence.
Action, not words, is the main thing, and
excessive talk leads to error and delusion.[39]

1:18
Rabban Shimon ben Gamliel teaches,

Three things ensure the world's survival:
justice, truth, and peace,[40]
as it is said,
"Speak truth, establish peace,
and render honest judgments in your
 gates."[41]

**1** Torah here refers to both the Written and Oral revelations given to Moses at Sinai. The Written became the basis for Priestly Judaism, and the Oral became the basis for Rabbinic Judaism. At the heart of Torah is ethical monotheism: One God manifesting one universe, one humanity, and one moral code rooted in justice, compassion, and humility.

**2** Exodus 24:12.

**3** Torah is received from a teacher and transmitted to a student. To receive you must be empty so as to make room for the teaching. To transmit you must be empty so as not to cling to what you received.

**4** The 120 members of the Great Assembly were called "great" because they saw the greatness of God manifest in all things (*Yoma* 69b).

**5** Judging is part of life, but certainty is not. Be humble in your judging and careful not to mistake hallowed opinion for sacred truth (see Deuteronomy 1:16–17).

**6** Teachers should raise students up on their shoulders that their vision may surpass that of their teachers. Do not transmit wisdom to replicate what you know, but to transcend it.

**7** A hedge is a living shield protecting what it surrounds. Traditionally this hedge is rabbinic law. Over time the law is confused with Torah, and an even thicker hedge of words is grown. But wisdom that comes from words alone is babble. Silence is the ultimate shield of Torah. In silence we can hear the Still Small Voice of God (1 Kings 19:12) and distinguish tribal norms from timeless truth. Do not hesitate to challenge the first in your pursuit of the second.

**8** Literally, Torah, worship, and loving-kindness. True Torah is wisdom: knowing that One God manifests as one world, one humanity, and one moral code—justice and compassion for all. True worship is surrender to God's will, that is, reality as it manifests in and as you at this and every moment. When you surrender to reality, you engage each moment and all that it brings with grace, humor, and thanksgiving. Hence Job's comment to his wife: "Shall we accept only good from God and not evil?" (Job 2:10). True loving-kindness is compassion toward self and other. When you awaken to wisdom and know reality as God's will, narrow mind *(mochin d'katnut)* yields to spacious mind *(mochin d'gadlut)* and you experience the greater *shlemut* (nonduality) that is God. This gives rise to an overwhelming sense of compassion for self and other in the infinite expanse of God.

**9** When you act for reward you focus not on the deed but on the doer. When there is no thought of reward, there is no thought of the doer. When there is no thought of doer, the deed is done with simplicity and grace. This is living with the awe of heaven.

**10** Bringing the wise into your home takes courage, for they will challenge all you hold dear. Those who come only to applaud are not wise, merely clever.

**11** To sit in the dust of the wise is to travel in their footsteps, follow their logic, and test their conclusions. But once you have walked their path, you must step off and see what is so for yourself. Wisdom cannot be secondhand.

**12** Jesus said, "I stood in the midst of the world, and I appeared to them in the flesh. I found them all drunk; I found none of them thirsting" (*Gospel According to Thomas,* 28). The narrow mind does not thirst for truth, for it is drunk on the cheap wine of desire, imagined sovereignty, and permanence. You have to sober up, see the world as it is, and then drink thirstily of wisdom.

**13** Rabbi Yose ben Yochanan's hospitality is more radical than his friend's, for he challenges you to open your house not only to the sages, but to the world. Do not imagine your home is a castle, a defense against the world. Rather, live without defenses, seeing everyone as family, sons and daughters of the Only One we call God.

**14** Idle chatter is the currency of narrow mind. The words are self-serving, impressing another to maintain the illusion of self. Speak without attention and you speak carelessly, shallowly, giving bad advice and falling easily into gossip. Flirtatious talk is the epitome of idle chatter, leading you into the hell of your own self-obsessed drama.

**15** Three things make you worthy of a teacher: the capacity to listen in the beginning, the ability to question in the middle, and the courage to go your own way in the end.

**16** A teacher shares what she knows; a friend helps clarify what you know. The Hebrew *k'nay,* here translated as "secure," literally means "to buy." What does a real friend cost? Absolute honesty.

**17** At some level everyone is a stranger to you, so do not presume you know all there is to know about someone. People do what they do because at that moment that is all they can do. Know this and you will judge everyone with compassion.

**18** A bad neighbor sows discord through gossip, slander, and lies. Stay away from these.

**19** Do not conspire to pervert the truth or exploit another, and in time justice will prevail, for evil cannot succeed alone.

**20** Do not despair because justice is slow; do justly yourself and work for justice in your community, and in the end evil will fall before it.

**21** When judging between ideas, people, or courses of action, consider all sides impartially; do not defend or attack one side or the other. See them both as flawed that you might see the good in each. And when the choice is made, see them both as good that you might remember the flaws in each. In this way you reject nothing even as you choose one thing.

**22** When investigating truth, do not settle for beloved opinions. Be careful that your words do not betray your desire and lead others to flatter rather than enlighten. The truths you desire feed what you already know. The truths you need free you from the known, that you might see what *is* without the filter of how you so desperately wish it to be.

**23** The work to which you are born is to till the soil that the earth might birth life (Genesis 2:5). What is the soil you are to till? The soil of self (Genesis 2:7), the dust that is your incarnate being. To till is to break up the hard-packed soil of *mochin d'katnut* (narrow mind) and let in the light and air of *mochin d'gadlut* (spacious mind). This is the work of meditation, prayer, chanting, deep dialogue, and contemplative study.

**24** Fear rests at the heart of both religion and politics, for both are obsessed with power and control. While church and state are capable of doing good, each is easily seduced into excusing great evil in the name of a greater good. The wise rest not in fear but in love and have no need for either power or control. If you pursue wisdom, beware of priests and politicians.

**25** Words are to truth what a menu is to a meal—pointers only and never the thing itself. Where words are mistaken for truth, cleverness passes for wisdom, and propaganda and passion overwhelm clarity and purpose. In such a place ideologies become more important than reality, and people drink from wells polluted by ignorance.

**26** The Name of Heaven, *Shem Shemayim,* refers to God's purpose. God's purpose is to manifest a world capable of knowing itself as God. To achieve this you must see what is. In the Zohar (Numbers 220b), the sacred text of Jewish mysticism, "what is" is called *koach-mah,* a play on the word *chochmah,* wisdom. To see what *is* is to be filled with wisdom. You lose this wisdom when you mistake talk for truth, and imagine the map is the territory or the menu is the meal. This is no longer wisdom, but idolatry, worshipping the *ism* rather than engaging the *Is.*

**27** God tells us the way of Aaron: "He walked with Me in peace and impartiality, and turned many from folly" (Malachi 2:6). To walk the way of Aaron is to take refuge in peace *(shalom),* wholeness *(shalem),* and nonduality *(shlemut).* Rooted in these you reject nothing and no one, seeing all things and everyone as part of God.

**28** It is not enough that you prefer peace to conflict; you must do all you can to bring peace about in the midst of conflict. As Jesus taught, "Blessed are the peacemakers, for they shall be called the children of God" (Matthew 5:9).

**29** Bringing people to Torah is not bringing them to religion, but to wisdom. It is one thing to convince others of what you know; it is quite another to step with them into what is unknown to you both.

**30** Fame raises you above others; honor raises others above yourself. The first distracts you from reality; the second reveals it to you.

**31** Knowledge is the known; wisdom is the unknown. The known is the past; the unknown is the timeless present. When you cling to the known, you live in the past: today imitates yesterday, and tomorrow replicates today. Living with wisdom is living in the present moment: no imitation, no replication, each moment new, fresh, and surprising.

**32** True learning is not memorizing what was, but staying open to what is. If you cease to learn, reality is replaced with memory, and all your living is counterfeit.

**33** Exploiting knowledge means living from the past, selling the known disguised as the unknown. This fills you with the illusion of control, robbing you of humility, compassion, grace, and any hope of experiencing wisdom.

**34** Being for yourself is honoring *mochin d'katnut,* the narrow mind of the relative self. Honoring narrow mind means seeing to the welfare of body, heart, and mind. No one can do this for you.

**35** Being for yourself alone dishonors narrow mind by forcing it to function in isolation, when in fact it is part of a greater unity. Imagining you are apart from the world makes you fearful of the world, placing you in a zero-sum delusion of scarcity that breeds anger, greed, violence, and injustice. Balancing being for yourself with being for others is living from *mochin d'gadlut,* the spacious mind that sees all things as part of the One. Living from spacious mind is living without fear and the anger, greed, violence, and injustice that fear carries with it.

**36** Past and future are ghosts. There is only now. If you would honor yourself and others, now is the only time you have to do so.

**37** These are not three teachings, but one: the Way of Wisdom is to say little and do much; welcoming everyone with grace, compassion, humility, and kindness; and seeing each and every one as a facet of the One and Only.

**38** A teacher offers a much-needed map, but you alone must walk the territory. Doubt that keeps you from testing the map is to be avoided. Doubt that keeps you from mistaking the map for the territory is to be embraced. Give justly, and do not excuse miserliness through guesswork.

**39** Silence trumps talk, for talk is always about the known, and the known is always about the past ... only silence allows you to rest in the present. Action trumps talk, for talk leads to the delusion of action; you imagine you are doing because you are talking about doing. It is not the thought that counts, and certainly not the talk about the thought. Practice rooted in silence is the way of the sage.

**40** A world without justice is a world run by fear. Fear gives rise to anger, anger to violence, and violence to even greater fear and injustice. A world without truth is a world driven by lies. Lies give rise to confusion, confusion to conflict, conflict to hatred, and hatred to even more lies. A world without peace is a world driven by division. Division gives rise to scarcity, scarcity to hoarding, and hoarding to genocide.

**41** Zechariah 8:16.

# Chapter Two

2:1
Rabbi[1] said, What is the right path?
One that honors both self and other.[2]

Be as mindful of small acts as great
 ones,
for you cannot know the consequences
 of either.

If you decide to act,
weigh the cost to you against the
 benefit to others.
If you decide not to act,
weigh the benefit to you against the
 cost to others.[3]

Sin's grip is loosened when three things
 are known:
the seeing eye,
the hearing ear,
and the Book of Record.[4]

2:2
Rabban Gamliel ben Rabbi Yehudah
 HaNasi teaches,

Engrossed in learning, engaged in work,
you forget the pangs of selfish desire.[5]
Learning without labor is barren and
 robs the world of your effort.[6]
Do not profit from community service.
If you promote the welfare of all,
you tap the merit of the community,
your efforts will endure,
and God will credit you as if you had
 acted alone.[7]

2:3
Beware the powerful; their friendship is
 a matter of convenience.
They will abandon you when it suits
 their purposes to do so.[8]

2:4
He says,
Align your will with God's will,
and God's will becomes your will.
Surrender your will to God's will,
and God will surrender others' will to
 your will.[9]

2:5
Hillel teaches,
Do not abandon community.[10]

Do not be certain of yourself until you die.[11]
Do not judge others until standing in their place.[12]
Do not abandon the new simply because it is new.[13]
Do not say, "When I am free I will study,"
for perhaps you will never be free.[14]

2:6
Hillel says,
The fearlessness of a fool is empty;[15]
the piety of a boor is hollow;[16]
the learning of the shy is shallow;[17]
the teaching of the impatient is trite.[18]
A scholar cannot be preoccupied with business.[19]
In a place where there is no hero, be a hero.[20]

2:7
Hillel saw a skull floating on the water. He said to it,
Because you drowned others, you have drowned;

and those who drowned you will themselves drown.[21]

## 2:8
Hillel used to say,
The more fat, the more disease.
The more possessions, the more worry.
The more wives, the more rivalry.
The more maids, the more frivolity.
The more butlers, the more theft.
[However]
The more Torah, the more life.
The more study, the more wisdom.
The more guidance, the more understanding.
The more generosity, the more peace.[22]
A good reputation will serve you in this world;
knowledge of Torah will serve you in the World to Come.[23]

## 2:9
Rabban Yochanan ben Zakkai received transmission from Hillel and Shammai.
He used to say,
Take no credit for your wisdom,
becoming wise is the reason you were born.[24]

2:10
Rabban Yochanan ben Zakkai had five key disciples:
Rabbi Eliezer ben Hyrkanos, Rabbi Yehoshua ben Chanania,
Rabbi Yose HaKohen, Rabbi Shimon ben Netanel,
and Rabbi Elazar ben Arach.

2:11
Each one had his gifts.
Rabbi Eliezer ben Hyrkanos is a tightly sealed cistern holding every drop.
Rabbi Yehoshua ben Chanania—praised is she who bore him![25]
Rabbi Yose HaKohen is pious in every detail.
Rabbi Shimon ben Netanel avoids every misstep.
Rabbi Elazar ben Arach is a spring whose flow only increases.

2:12
Rabban Yochanan ben Zakkai used to say,
Place all the sages of Israel on one pan of a balance-scale
and Eliezer ben Hyrkanos on the other, he would outweigh them all.

According to Abba Shaul, he also said,
If all the sages of Israel including
 Eliezer ben Hyrkanos were on one pan,
and Rabbi Elazar ben Arach were alone
 in the other,
he would outweigh them all.

## 2:13
Rabban Yochanan ben Zakkai said to
 his disciples,
Look and see: What is the key to right
 action?
Rabbi Eliezer: A good eye.[26]
Rabbi Yehoshua: A good friend.[27]
Rabbi Yose: A good neighbor.[28]
Rabbi Shimon: A good mind.[29]
Rabbi Elazar: A good heart.[30]
Rabban Yochanan ben Zakkai said to
 them,
I prefer the words of Elazar ben Arach,
for his words include your words.

## 2:14
Rabban Yochanan ben Zakkai said to
 his disciples,
Look and see: What is the key to wrong
 action?
Rabbi Eliezer: An evil eye.[31]

Rabbi Yehoshua: An evil friend.[32]
Rabbi Yose: An evil neighbor.[33]
Rabbi Shimon: One who steals under the pretext of borrowing.[34]
Every borrowing is borrowing from God, as it is said,
"The wicked one borrows and does not repay,
but the Righteous One is gracious and gives."[35]
Rabbi Elazar: An evil heart.[36]
Rabban Yochanan ben Zakkai said to them,
I prefer the words of Elazar ben Arach, for his words include your words.

2:15
The disciples of Rabban Yochanan ben Zakkai each teach three things.

Rabbi Eliezer teaches,
Let another's honor be as dear to you as your own.
Be slow to anger, and return[37] one day before you die.[38]
Be warmed by the sages' fire,
but beware being burned by their embers.[39]

They bite like a fox,
sting like a scorpion,
hiss like a snake,
and all their words are white-hot coals.[40]

2:16
Rabbi Yehoshua teaches,
An eye obsessed with evil,
a will obsessed with self,
and hatred of others
drives you from the world.[41]

2:17
Rabbi Yose teaches,
Protect another's possessions as you
 would your own.
Seek out wisdom for yourself, and don't
 rely on inherited truth.[42]
Do all you do for the sake of heaven.[43]

2:18
Rabbi Shimon ben Netanel teaches,
Be mindful reciting the *Sh'ma* and be
 attentive in prayer.[44]
Do not pray from rote,
but seek compassion and surrender
 before God,[45]
as it is said,

"For God is gracious, compassionate,
 slow to anger,
abounding in kindness,
and resentful of punishment."[46]
Do not despair when left to your own
 devices.[47]

## 2:19
Rabbi Elazar [ben Arach] teaches,
Be diligent in Torah, and know how to
 answer the challenger.[48]
Know before Whom you study,[49]
and know that reward is linked to
 effort.[50]

## 2:20
Rabbi Tarfon teaches,
The day is short.
The task is long.
The workers are lazy.
The stakes are high.
The Master is demanding.[51]

## 2:21
Rabbi Tarfon also says,
You are not obligated to complete the
 task,
nor are you free to abandon it.[52]

If you have studied much Torah
you will reap great reward.
You can rely on your Employer to pay
 you your due,
but not in the currency of this world,
but rather the World to Come.⁵³

**1** "Rabbi" refers to Yehudah HaNasi, Judah the Prince, who compiled the Mishnah, the early teachings of the Oral Law, shortly before his death in 217CE.

**2** What is the right path? One that honors the senses, celebrates love, promotes reason, affirms diversity, and recognizes unity.

**3** Both action and nonaction have consequences. Before choosing one way or the other, look carefully to see what these may be to both yourself and others. If the benefit to others is greater than the cost to you, do it. If the benefit to you outweighs the cost to others, think again.

**4** Sin is rooted in selfishness, and selfishness is the result of narrow mind out of touch with spacious mind. To cultivate spacious mind, practice seeing not only to the needs of self but to the needs of others, hearing not only the clamor of self but the anguish of others; and remember that selfish acts will haunt you all your life.

**5** Selfishness emerges from an idle self, for an idle self makes an idol of the self.

**6** There is only one question you need ask to judge yourself: Have you made the world a better place for your having been born into it?

**7** Working for the welfare of the community aligns the community behind you, strengthening your efforts and maximizing results. And while your success will depend on the support of the community, the credit will be yours nonetheless.

**8** People in power have only one desire: remain in power. Do not imagine you can benefit from their largess, for it is you who serves their pleasure and not they who serve yours.

**9** God's will is reality, the way things are at this very moment. Aligning with God's will means working with what is rather than what you wish things to be. Surrendering your will to God's will means acting in accord with reality. If you do, others will follow suit, and you will be of one Mind.

**10** No matter how unjust the world may seem, your task is to move it toward justice.

**11** The human hunger for certainty is so great that it will accept almost any delusion. Question yourself and your motives. The humility of not-knowing is your greatest defense against the arrogance of false-knowing.

**12** Actions arise from conditions. Do not judge the former until you understand the latter.

**13** Wisdom is often at odds with accepted knowledge. Test what you know, and let reality rather than mass appeal reveal what is true.

**14** Do not hope to find time to study; time is never found, only made.

**15** Courage that arises from ignorance is not courage, but foolishness. Fear is not the enemy; acquiescing to fear is the enemy.

**16** Piety that arises from conformity is soulless. Imitate God, the Unconditioned, not your neighbor.

**17** Learning without bold questioning is rote. Don't ask your children what they have learned; ask what they have asked.

**18** Teaching without thoughtful consideration is proselytizing. Don't ask your teachers what they know, but what they don't know.

**19** If you worry more about making a dollar than making a difference, you will probably end up with neither.

**20** A hero is one who speaks for the silenced (Proverbs 31:8). Do not collaborate with immorality, even if the majority calls it moral.

**21** How you act in this moment sets the conditions for what you will encounter in the next moment. Your behavior is yours to control; the results of your behavior are outside your control. Influence conditions by aligning your actions with justice and compassion. Deeds fashion destiny. The heaven you desire and the hell you fear are both in your hands.

**22** *Mochin d'katnut* (narrow mind) lives under the delusion of scarcity; salvation lies with having more: more stuff, more faith, more power, more control. Having more is the real religion of narrow mind. *Mochin d'gadlut* (spacious mind) lives in a world characterized by abundance. There is always enough as long as you are free from the compulsion for more. Narrow mind is about having; spacious mind is about being. Hillel is not opposed to possessions, only to being possessed by them.

**23** "This world" is the world of narrow mind whose currency is a good reputation, proving that you can own without being owned and have without being had. The World to Come is the world of spacious mind whose currency is Torah, wisdom; seeing the world as it is without the delusions of ideology, nationalism, ethnicity, race, gender, religion. When you see what is, you act in harmony with it.

**24** You are the way God comes to know the world as godly. Taking credit for this is like taking credit for growing your fingernails.

**25** The Jerusalem Talmud reports that when Rabbi Yehoshua was an infant, his mother would carry him to the local school that his ears might grow accustomed to Torah. Henceforth, whenever he is mentioned, his wisdom is credited to his mother (*Yevamot* 1:6).

**26** A good eye sees through delusion to truth.

**27** A good friend challenges you to be your best.

**28** A good neighbor honors you and what is yours.

**29** A good mind weighs the consequences of an act before doing that act, thus avoiding unnecessary suffering.

**30** A good heart desires only what is right and true for both self and other and thus includes the best traits of all the rest.

**31** An evil eye sees what it wants to see in order to excuse what it wants to do.

**32** An evil friend values you as a means to be exploited, not as an end to be respected.

**33** An evil neighbor seeks status by spreading discord through gossip and slander.

**34** This one steals not only possessions, but loyalty and reputations as well, using you to cause suffering to others.

**35** Psalm 37:21.

**36** An evil heart excuses evil deeds and thus includes the worst traits of all the rest.

**37** The Hebrew word *teshuvah,* "return," is usually translated as "repent," from the Old French, *repentir,* "to be sorry." While not inaccurate, it is insufficient. *Teshuvah* is more than remorse. *Teshuvah* uses remorse to return to your true nature as the image and likeness of God. The very fact that you feel sorry means you are reconnecting to your innate goodness.

**38** Since you cannot know when you will die, returning to your true nature through prayer and meditation must be a constant process.

**39** The sages' fire is their wisdom, but even this can be perverted when ideas become idols. Learn what you can, but do not worship what you learn.

**40** When sages engage in opening you to truth, the experience is anything but comforting. They bite like a fox, cleverly teasing out your most cherished ideas that they can rip them from you. They sting like a scorpion, killing the idols of narrow mind with sudden insight into their vacuity. They hiss like a snake, keeping you away from all your hiding places. All their words are white-hot coals, burning away all you know and leaving you raw before the real.

**41** This world is the world of relationship, of I and Thou, self and other. It is a world dependent on balance, interdependence, and harmony. If you focus only on yourself, you treat the world as an It, a means toward your own ends; in so doing you isolate yourself from others and exile yourself from the world.

**42** Truth is dynamic, arising from reality in the moment. Hence truth cannot be inherited from the past. There is no need to forget the past; just don't expect it to be true in the present.

**43** Acting for the sake of heaven is acting for the good of the whole.

**44** The *Sh'ma* (literally, "The Hearing"), "Hear, O Israel, Y-H-V-H is our God, Y-H-V-H is One" (Deuteronomy 6:4), is Judaism's affirmation of nonduality. All is one in, with, and as God. While self-evident to spacious mind, the message of the *Sh'ma* is lost on narrow mind, which sees the world's diversity at the expense of its greater nonduality. The intent of the *Sh'ma* is to shift you from narrow mind to spacious mind. It must be said with full attention if the shift is to happen.

**45** The purpose of prayer is to cultivate compassion and surrender to Truth. Compassion and surrender are spontaneous, a gift of grace rather than the result of habit. Prayer that becomes rote is imitative and thus incapable of achieving its goals.

**46** Joel 2:13.

**47** To despair is to be without *(dis)* hope *(sperare)*. You lose hope when you imagine you are other than the whole, separate (dis-paired) from the One who manifests the many. This is the state of narrow mind cut off from the greater truth of spacious mind, the interdependence of all things in, with, and as God. The key to despair is repair, becoming whole *(shalem)* by awakening to God's nonduality *(shlemut)*.

**48** One who knows the truth is never angered by another's questions or opinions. When people challenge you, answer with compassion, and invite them to see what is and not what you or they imagine should be.

**49** For the Rabbis, study is a means for shifting from narrow mind to spacious mind. Do not study absent-mindedly, but be aware of the Greater One opening in you, as you.

**50** The reward for study is awakening to spacious mind and returning to your true nature as the image and likeness of God. This is not a matter of quantity, but quality. The effort is what turns you, not the knowledge gained from it.

**51** This is Rabbi Tarfon's analogy of the spiritual quest. The day is short, there is only this moment; the task is long, for the distance between narrow mind and spacious mind appears immense; the workers are lazy, the challenge of turning seems too great; the stakes are high, the very salvation of person and planet depends upon it; the Master is demanding, God accepts nothing but the whole. Hesitate and you are lost.

**52** Having frightened his students with the previous teaching, Rabbi Tarfon softens it with this one: While the task is long and the time is short, you are not obligated to complete it. Effort alone is what matters.

**53** The reward for returning to your true nature is not wealth or power, self-esteem or fame, but the ability to see the part in the whole and thus escape the fear, anger, violence, and greed that come with imagining you are apart from rather than a part of God.

# Chapter Three

3:1
Akavia ben Mahalalel teaches,
Reflect on three things and come to no harm:
where you come from;
where you are going;
and to Whom you are to give account.[1]

Where do you come from?
From a bitter drop of sperm.
Where are you going?
To dust, worms, and maggots.
To Whom are you to give account?
To the One Who cannot be deceived.[2]

3:2
Rabbi Chanina ben Tradyon,
the deputy High Priest, teaches,
Pray for the peace of the government,
for without it the people would eat each other alive.[3]

3:3
Rabbi Chanina ben Tradyon teaches,

When two sit together without sharing
 words of Torah,
their talk turns to foolishness.[4] Hence it
 says,
"Do not sit among a gathering of
 fools."[5]

When two sit together and share words
 of Torah,
the *Shechinah* rests between them.[6]
Hence it says, "Then those who fear
 God spoke to one another,
and God listened and heard, and a book
 of remembrance
was written before God for those who
 fear God
and give thought to God's Name."[7]

This applies to one as well as two:[8] "Let
 one sit in solitude and be still,
for he will have received [a reward] for
 doing so."[9]

3:4
Rabbi Shimon [ben Netanel] teaches,
If three eat together and share no
 Torah,
theirs is a feast for idols.[10] Hence it says,

"Without God, all tables are full of vomit and filth."[11]
But if three eat together and share Torah,
theirs is a feast with God.[12] Hence it says,
"And he said to me, 'This is God's table.'"[13]

3:5
Rabbi Chanina ben Chachinai teaches,
When alone at night
or walking solitary on a road
do not let your thoughts run wild,
for they will turn against you.[14]

3:6
Rabbi Nechunya ben Hakanah teaches,
Devotion to Torah frees you from power and possessions.
Ignore Torah and they will crush you.[15]

3:7
Rabbi Chalafta ben Dosa of Kfar Chanania teaches,
If ten people sit together and study Torah,

the *Shechinah* rests among them. Hence it says,
"God stands in the assembly of the godly."[16]
This is also true of five, for it says,
"God has established God's bundle on earth."[17]
It is also true of three, for it says,
"In the midst of judges God shall judge."[18]
It is also true of two, for it says,
"Then the God-intoxicated spoke to one another,
and God listened and heard."[19]
This is even true of one, for it says,
"In every place where I cause My Name to be mentioned,
I will come to you and bless you."[20,21]

3:8
Rabbi Elazar of Bartosa teaches,
Give God only what is God's,
for you and all you have are God's.[22]
So David said,
"For everything is from You,
and from Your Own we are giving You."[23]

**3:9**
Rabbi Yaakov teaches,
If you walk on the road absorbed in Torah
and place words between this and that, saying,
"How beautiful this tree! How wonderful this plowed field!"—
you have lost your soul.[24]

**3:10**
Rabbi Dostai bar Yannai teaches in the name of Rabbi Meir,
If you forget wisdom, your soul suffers.[25]
Hence it says,
"Guard your soul from forgetting what your eyes have seen."[26]
Yet to forget is natural; are we punished for poor memory?
No, Torah refers only to those who devote their days to denying wisdom.[27]
Hence Torah goes on to say,
"Lest they be removed from your heart all the days of your life."[28]

**3:11**
Rabbi Chanina ben Dosa teaches,

If your concern for others exceeds your desire for wisdom,
your wisdom will endure.
If your desire for wisdom exceeds your concern for others,
your wisdom will not endure.[29]

**3:12**
He also said,
If your kindness exceeds your wisdom,
your wisdom will endure.
If your wisdom exceeds your kindness,
your wisdom will not endure.[30]

**3:13**
And he said,
If you bring joy to others, God rejoices in you.
If you bring no joy to others, God does not rejoice in you.[31]

**3:14**
Rabbi Dosa ben Harkinas teaches,
Sleeping late,
drinking early,
screeching children,
and the babble of fools will drive you out of the world.[32]

3:15
Rabbi Elazar the Moda'ite teaches,
If you mock the sacred,
disgrace the Festivals,[33]
humiliate people in public,
deny your heritage,
or pit Torah against tradition,
even study and kindness
will not secure you a place in the World to Come.[34]

3:16
Rabbi Yishmael teaches,
Yield to the stronger,[35]
maintain your composure among the young,[36]
and welcome every person with joy.[37]

3:17
Rabbi Akiva teaches,
Mockery and cynicism lead to wickedness.[38]
Tradition protects truth;
generosity protects wealth;
intention protects abstinence;
silence protects wisdom.[39]

3:18

He used to say,
You are loved, for you are created in God's image.
This love is greater still for it being revealed to you:[40]
"For in the image of God, God made *adam*."[41]
Israel is loved, for they are the Children of the Place.[42]
This love is greater still for it being revealed to them:
"You are children to *HaShem* your God."[43]
Israel is loved for they were given the precious tool, as it says,
"For I have given you a good teaching; do not forsake My Torah."[44]

3:19
Everything is foreseen,
yet freedom of choice is given.[45]
The world is judged by goodness,
and everything depends upon unbounded kindness.[46]

3:20
He used to say,
Everything is on loan,[47]

and a net envelops all the living.[48]
The shop is open;
the Merchant extends credit;
the ledger is open;
the hand writes;
and whoever wishes to borrow, come and borrow.
The collectors make their rounds constantly, day-by-day,
collecting payment whether you know it or not.
They do not act capriciously;
their judgments are just;[49]
and everything is in service to the final banquet.[50]

3:21
Rabbi Elazar ben Azariah teaches,
Without the sacred, there is no mundane;
without the mundane there is no sacred.[51]
Without wisdom there is no wonder;
without wonder there is no wisdom.[52]
Without awareness there is no understanding;
without understanding there is no awareness.[53]

Without flour there is no Torah;
without Torah there is no flour.[54]

3:22
He used to say:
If your wisdom exceeds your kindness,
you are like a tree whose branches are
 many and whose roots are few.
Even a slight breeze will topple you.[55]
As it says,
"And he shall be like an isolated tree
 in an arid land
and shall not see when good comes;
he shall swell on parched soil in the
 wilderness,
on a salted land, uninhabited."[56]
If your kindness exceeds your wisdom,
you are like a tree whose branches are
 few and whose roots are many.
Even if all the winds of the world were
 to blow against you,
still you would not budge.[57]
As it says,
"And he shall be like a tree planted by
 waters,
toward the stream spreading its roots,
and it shall not notice the heat's arrival,
and its foliage shall be fresh;

in the year of drought it shall not worry,

nor shall it cease from yielding fruit."⁵⁸

3:23
Rabbi Eliezer ben Chisma teaches,
Even seemingly minor laws
such as those regarding bird-offerings
and the start of a woman's menstrual cycle
are wells of wisdom
for one who knows how to drink from them.
Astronomy and mathematics are like seasonings
to the meal that is Torah.⁵⁹

**1** Hasidic Jews have a saying: People should carry two slips of paper with them at all times. On one is written, "You are the reason the world was created." On the other, "You are nothing but dust and ash." When you forget your true identity as God manifest, read the first. When you mistake yourself for someone special, read the second. In this way you avoid falling into the traps of self-negation and megalomania.

**2** On the one hand, you are nothing but sperm and egg, a vehicle for transmitting genetic code from one generation to another. On the other, you are to worms what a beef cow may be to you—lunch. And yet you are held accountable to God, the Undeceivable. Why? Because everything matters to God. Why? Because everything is God. You are the way God writes symphonies and bad checks. You are the way God cries over newborns and last breaths. You are the way God is God as you. It is you to whom God points and says to the worms, "This is my body." It is you to whom God points and says to the fleas, "This is my blood." You are the way God eats and is eaten. Do not be deceived: you are nothing more and nothing less. How marvelous!

**3** Rabbi Chanina was no anarchist believing that left to our own devices we humans would naturally do justly, love mercy, and walk humbly. On the contrary, he believed that if not for the external restraints of law, and the police and courts to enforce the law, people would turn on one another, and greed and violence would define us exclusively.

It is interesting to note that it is the priest who fears the people. Interesting, perhaps, but not surprising. Priests owe their authority to fear, more specifically to the people's fear of God. If God were not fearsome, people would have no need for priests, whose job it is to keep the people safe from God through ritual and sacrifice. The priests scare the people, and the people scare the priests.

But is Chanina right? Does the law keep you honest? Would you suddenly go wild if there were no one to stop you? Or would you live pretty much as you do already? There is a place for government and law, but without it would we all become predators?

**4** Wisdom emerges from the meeting of thoughtful people. Sitting with another human being is an opportunity to challenge and be challenged, to open up to new ideas, and to see the world in new ways. Wasting this opportunity through idle chatter is denying the value of both self and other.

**5** Psalm 1:1.

**6** *Shechinah* is the Presence of God. Notice that it rests between them and not upon them. God is realized in the emptiness just outside the narrow mind of each person.

**7** Malachi 3:16. Giving thought to God's Name refers to the practice of *gerushin,* ceaselessly chanting a Name of God such as *HaRachaman* (the Compassionate One) or Allah, Krishna,

Ram, or Jesus. Chanting God's Name is a universal practice found in all religions, and is one of the easiest ways to open narrow mind to spacious mind. And when you do, you are re-membered, made whole *(shalem)* in the nonduality *(shlemut)* of God.

**8** You cannot be alone, for you are part of the All One. Sitting still in solitude removes the delusion of isolation and aloneness and reveals the all-embracing unity that is God.

**9** Lamentations 3:28.

**10** Rabbi Shimon expands on Rabbi Chanina's teaching by adding the dimension of food. Sharing a meal together is an opportunity to share wisdom as well, but too often it is a time for self-aggrandizement and one-upmanship, worshiping the idol of self rather than opening to the wisdom of God.

**11** Isaiah 28:8.

**12** Notice "with God" rather than "of God." God is with them in their meeting. People cannot meet one another as *mochin d'katnut,* "narrow mind," for narrow mind simply projects itself onto the other and meets nothing but a fun-house mirror image of itself. True meeting happens from spacious mind, mind open to wonder and diversity; mind open to nonduality rather than conformity; mind that honors the narrow self even as it realizes the greater Self that is God.

**13** Ezekiel 41:22.

**14** Alone, the narrow mind naturally wanders, grasping at thoughts and spinning dramas that blot out your truer identity as spacious mind. Do not seek to control the mind, for the controller is only the same mind pretending to difference. Rather, choose not to chase the wandering thought. Without you to chase it, it will not run away, but fade away. If you need something to do instead of chasing your thoughts, practice *gerushin* (from *l'garesh,* "to separate"), the practice of repeating a Name of God or sacred phrase in order to separate yourself from destructive thoughts and behaviors.

**15** Power and possessions are the currency of narrow mind, the means by which it maintains the delusion of its separateness from God. Torah opens narrow mind to spacious mind, not negating the preciousness of self, but placing it in the larger context of God's nonduality. Without the freedom of spacious mind, narrow mind collapses under the weight of its own delusion.

**16** Psalm 82:1.

**17** Amos 9:6. "Bundle" refers to what can be grasped by the five fingers of a hand.

**18** Psalm 82:1. Jewish courts required three-judge panels.

**19** Malachi 3:16.

**20** Exodus 20:21.

**21** In Judaism, ten people constitute a *minyan,* a prayer quorum. The number ten hearkens back to Abraham arguing for the salvation of Sodom by getting God to spare the city for the sake of ten righteous people (Genesis 18:32). It was thought that ten was the minimum number of people needed to effect a positive change in society. Knowing that Sodom fell for lack of ten, Rabbi Chalafta says even five can suffice. Fearing that even five may not be found, he finds evidence for the power of three, and then two. Yet even here he is not willing to rest, for even one person in touch with God has the potential to transform the world for the better, as Abraham, Moses, Jesus, and Mohammed attest.

**22** Predating similar remarks by Jesus in Mark 22:21 and Luke 20:25, Rabbi Elazar is speaking from the perspective of spacious mind, knowing that all is God. Everything you are and have is God; you own nothing. Thus treat all things as on loan, and prepare to return them to their Source in good condition and without regret.

**23** 1 Chronicles 29:14.

**24** When you first encounter the beauty of a tree there are no words. There is silent wonder. Spacious mind is present in wonder, not words. Your soul, your true nature as spacious mind, is lost when the wonder slips into words. To speak of the tree is to no longer commune with it. Its presence is past, and you glorify only memory. Do not rush to articulate wonder. Simply stand in its presence.

**25** You are born knowing the Truth of God's nonduality. You know it right now: you are a part of and not apart from the One Who Is All. Spacious mind knows this intrinsically. It is not learned, nor can it be forgotten. But narrow mind denies this truth and in so doing feeds its delusion of sovereignty. The effort to deny what you know harms your soul, your innate spaciousness, and leaves narrow mind anxious and afraid.

**26** Deuteronomy 4:9.

**27** Rabbi Dostai isn't worried about the natural forgetfulness to which each of us is heir. His concern is with deliberate acts of forgetting and denying the truth.

**28** Deuteronomy 4:9. While it may seem otherwise, forgetting is more difficult than remembering. Forgetting requires a body impervious to ecstasy, remembering only a fleeting kiss from a beloved. Forgetting demands a heart hard and brittle, remembering only a moment's cry of joy. Forgetting requires constant denial of God, remembering only a moment of surrender. Forgetting demands ceaseless hiding from the Other, remembering only an accidental meeting.

**29** Wisdom is not the supreme good and is held second to just engagement with others. Any insights you may gather at the expense of others will not last.

**30** Justice is not held higher than compassion, so Rabbi Chanina adds this statement to his previous one. Justice and compassion together must exceed the desire for wisdom, and no knowledge gained at their expense will survive.

**31** Better even than the pursuit of wisdom is the bringing of joy. Wisdom can bring you to the knowledge of God; joy brings you into the presence of God.

**32** Being in the world demands engagement, intention, and attention. Sleeping late avoids the first, drinking early dulls the second, and crying babies and babbling fools erase the third. Wake early, drink little and late, comfort the children, and teach silence to fools. In this way you may engage the world with fullness of body, heart, and mind.

**33** The Festivals are the three pilgrimage festivals of Pesach (Passover), Shavuot (Weeks), and Sukkot (Booths). Pesach marks the Exodus from Egypt, Shavuot commemorates the giving of the Torah on Mount Sinai, and Sukkot reminds us of the Israelites' forty years of wandering in the wilderness.

**34** For all their celebration of wisdom and kindness, honoring others is still considered the highest virtue by the sages. Even if you are not moved by the practices of others, do not mock them. Even if your family's customs no longer appeal to you, do not refuse to participate in them. Even if your understanding of Torah challenges the traditions others hold dear, do not denigrate them. Being true to yourself does not secure your place in the World to Come; only being true to Truth can do that.

**35** Be like water, finding the course of least resistance. Do not pick a fight you know you cannot win.

**36** Do not succumb to silliness or become angry over the indiscretions of youth. You honor the young by allowing them to be young, not by imitating or admonishing them.

**37** Just as the sky is not troubled by the storm cloud and the ocean is not disturbed by the wave, be open to all that is, and welcome it with the equanimity of spacious mind that knows it is all God.

**38** When you mock others, you reduce them to objects for your own exploitation. Living beings become means to your ends rather than valuable ends in and of themselves.

**39** Tradition protects truth by translating truth into action; generosity protects wealth by freeing you from greed and scarcity thinking; intention protects abstinence by placing it in service to something greater than itself; silence protects wisdom by rooting it in not knowing rather than not wanting others to know.

**40** Spacious mind knows it is God's image, but for this wisdom to matter in the relative world of seemingly separate things, it must be made known to narrow mind as well. The sacred scriptures of the world's religions are one way in which narrow mind is pointed in the direction of this realization.

**41** Genesis 9:6. Usually translated as "man," the Hebrew *adam* is more accurately rendered "earthling," from *adamah,* "earth." Humans (from *humus,* "earth") are the way nature becomes aware of "herself" as God, and God becomes aware of "himself" as Nature.

**42** A common name for God used by the sages is *HaMakom,* "the Place." God is the place of the world, the field in which all things arise and return. To realize you are a child of the Place is to realize your true nature as an extension of God in time and space.

**43** Deuteronomy 14:1. *HaShem,* "the Name," is a standard euphemism for the Tetragrammaton, the four-letter Name of God often and unfortunately translated as "Lord." The real Name, Y-H-V-H, is a variation on the Hebrew verb "to be." God is not a being, not even the Supreme Being, but *being* itself.

**44** Proverbs 4:2. Torah is a tool for tilling the soil of narrow mind to let in the light and spirit of spacious mind. Torah that does not break up the narrow mind is not God's Torah.

**45** From the perspective of narrow mind, free will is a given. We choose this or that, and our moral responsibility rests on this ability to choose. But from the perspective of spacious mind there is no free will: you see clearly what needs to be done, and you do it not by choice or compulsion but simply because it is what needs to be done. Everything is foreseen in spacious mind, yet narrow mind still holds on to the illusion of choice.

**46** Divine judgment rests not on the mistakes you make, but on the acts of kindness you do. Mistakes are made from ignorance: narrow mind's inability to see what needs to be done leads to choices that are often harmful to you and others. The value of life comes not from narrow mind but from spacious mind, the mind that acts choicelessly to bring out the compassion inherent in each moment.

**47** Life is on loan: receive all that is given, and do not pretend to choice or ownership.

**48** You are a knot of God's infinitely knotted net, never apart from and always a part of the One Who Is All.

**49** Reality allows you to do as you will, for good and for bad, and every deed has its consequence. Live justly and with compassion, and your life will be filled with meaning, purpose, integrity, and joy. Live through lies and cruelty, and your life will be filled with fear and plagued by anger, greed, and violence.

**50** Heaven and hell are a single feast, with everyone seated at a grand table overflowing with the finest food and drink. The only rule is this: you must use the utensils provided, each being six feet in length. Those who attempt to feed themselves with these tools starve, for they cannot maneuver the tools to reach their own mouths. Those who learn to feed others are themselves fed in turn. The first are in hell, the second in heaven, but the feast is common to them both.

**51** Sacred and mundane are not separate realities, but different sides of the one reality. Like up and down, in and out, tall and short, back and front, convex and concave, sacred and mundane are unique but not separate. Learning to see duality as part of a greater nonduality is key to living well.

**52** "The beginning of wisdom is the wonder of God" (Proverbs 9:10). Wisdom is the intuitive grasping of what is (*koach-mah* in Hebrew, a pun on *chochmah,* "wisdom" [*Zohar,* Numbers 220b]). There is a moment just prior to this insight in which the narrow mind is completely overwhelmed and empty. This is the moment of wonder that allows the insights of spacious mind to manifest.

**53** Awareness, *da'at,* refers to the awareness of the presence of God in, with, and as all things. Without this you cannot appreciate the true nature of things. Yet without the capacity to see things as seemingly separate entities, the diversity of God is lost. Both are needed if the nonduality *(shlemut)* of God is to be realized.

**54** "Flour" is a euphemism for earning a living. Torah that is not grounded in the contingencies of the relative world is irrelevant to that world. Yet flour alone, work without wisdom and wonder, is purposeless and exhausting. The two must go together.

**55** Your strength comes not from what you know, but from how well you live. A life rooted in abstractions and speculations will fall at the first stirring of the winds of sorrow. You will be without friends, empty and without love.

**56** Jeremiah 17:6.

**57** Your strength comes from what you do, not what you know. If your life is rooted in acts of love and kindness, your friendships are many and your life is moist and rich. When trouble comes you may bend, but you will not break.

**58** Jeremiah 17:8.

**59** No *mitzvah* (commandment) is minor when you understand its power to lift you beyond yourself. No *torah* (teaching) is useless when you understand its power to transform the self. No deed is beneath you when you understand what needs to be done. No science is denied when you understand the purpose of salt.

# Chapter Four

4:1
Ben Zoma teaches,
Who is wise?
One who learns from everyone, for it says,[1]
"From all my teachers I grew wise."[2]
Who is strong?
One who subdues oneself, for it says,[3]
"Patience is better than strength,
and self-control is superior to controlling armies."[4]
Who is rich?
One who loves what is, for it says,[5]
"Praise and contentment belong to those who eat from their own labor."[6]
You are praised in this world, and content in the World to Come.
Who is honored?
One who honors others, for it says,[7]
"Those who honor Me are honored;
and those who scorn Me are degraded."[8]

4:2
Ben Azzai teaches,
Race to do even a small kindness,

and run even faster to avoid sin.
One kindness leads to another kindness,
and one sin leads to another sin.
The consequence of kindness is more kindness;
the consequence of sin is more sin.[9]

**4:3**
He used to teach,
Scorn no one, and mock nothing,
for no one is without her hour,
and no thing without its place.[10]

**4:4**
Rabbi Levitas of Yavneh teaches,
Be increasingly humble in spirit,
for the hope of humankind is the worm.[11]

**4:5**
Rabbi Yochanan ben Beroka teaches,
Even if you desecrate the Name in secret,
your punishment will be public;
will and accident are the same regarding the desecration of the Name.[12]

**4:6**

Rabbi Yishmael bar Rabbi Yose teaches,
If you study Torah in order to teach
 Torah,
you will be given the means to study
 and teach.
If you study Torah in order to practice
 Torah,
you will be given the means to study,
 teach, observe, and practice.[13]

4:7
Rabbi Tzadok teaches,
Do not abandon the community.
When acting as judge, do not attack or
 defend.
Do not use the Torah for
 self-aggrandizement,
nor as a means for wealth or power.
As Hillel teaches, one who exploits
 Torah will fade away.
From this we know that using learning
 for personal gain and power
removes you from the world.[14]

4:8
Rabbi Yose teaches,
Honor Torah and people will respect
 you.

Disgrace Torah and you will be disgraced.[15]

**4:9**
Rabbi Yishmael bar Rabbi Yose teaches,
One who shuns judgment is free from jealousy, theft, and self-deception.[16]
One who is quick to judge is chased by these
and dies an arrogant fool.[17]

**4:10**
Rabbi Yishmael ben Rabbi Yose used to teach,
If called to judge, do not judge alone, for only God judges alone.[18]
If you render an opinion, do not insist it be followed,
for that choice rests with the majority.[19]

**4:11**
Rabbi Yonatan teaches,
If you live Torah when poor,
you will live Torah when rich.
If you neglect Torah when rich,
you will neglect Torah when poor.[20]

**4:12**

Rabbi Meir teaches,
Work less; study more.[21]
Be humble before everyone.
More work means more competitors.
Labor in Torah and God will grant you
 ample reward.[22]

4:13
Rabbi Eliezer ben Yaakov teaches,
Every kindness protects you;
every cruelty persecutes you.
Turning and kindness shield against
 misadventure.[23]

4:14
Rabbi Yochanan the Sandal Maker
 teaches,
Align with heaven and your efforts will
 endure.
Align against heaven and your efforts
 will fail.[24]

4:15
Rabbi Elazar ben Shamua teaches,
Teachers! Honor your students as you
 honor yourselves.
Friends! Honor your colleagues as you
 honor your teachers.

Students! Honor your teachers as you honor God.[25]

4:16
Rabbi Yehudah teaches,
Be mindful in your study,
for a careless teaching
is as dangerous as a willful sin.[26]

4:17
Rabbi Shimon teaches,
There are three crowns to which people aspire:
the crown of scholarship,
the crown of priesthood,
and the crown of royalty,
but the crown of a good name surpasses them all.[27]

4:18
Rabbi Nehorai teaches,
Move to a place of learning,
and do not assume that you can learn by yourself.
Wisdom comes from shared struggle,[28]
as it says,
"Do not rely on your understanding alone."[29]

4:19
Rabbi Yannai teaches,
No one can fathom the peace of the wicked
or the suffering of the just.[30]

4:20
Rabbi Matya ben Charash teaches,
Be the first to greet another.[31]
Be the tail of a lion, rather than the head of a fox.[32]

4:21
Rabbi Yaakov teaches,
This world is the gateway to the World to Come.
Prepare yourself here for the feast that is there.[33]

4:22
Rabbi Yaakov also teaches,
An hour of turning and kindness here outweighs eternity in the World to Come.[34]
An hour of ecstasy in the World to Come
outweighs time in this world.[35]

4:23
Rabbi Shimon ben Elazar teaches,
Don't cool another's anger in the midst of rage.
Don't console the bereaved while their dead lie before them.
Don't question the intention of one whose vow is already made.
Don't seek out a friend whose shame still stings.[36]

4:24
Shmuel HaKattan teaches,
Don't applaud your enemy's fall,
nor rejoice as he stumbles.
God's anger will turn
and the other's fate will be yours.[37]

4:25
Elisha ben Avuya teaches,
A child's learning is like ink on fresh paper.
A elder's learning is like ink on smudged paper.[38]

4:26
Rabbi Yose bar Yehudah of Kfar HaBavli teaches,

Learning Torah from the young
is like chewing unripe grapes
and drinking fresh wine.
Learning Torah from the old
is like chewing ripe grapes
and drinking fine aged wine.[39]

4:27
Rabbi Meir teaches,
Do not look at the vessel,
but at what it contains.
Some new bottles may hold aged wine,
while some old bottles may not even
contain new wine.[40]

4:28
Rabbi Elazar HaKappar teaches,
Jealousy, lust, and fame remove you
from the world.[41]

4:29
Rabbi Elazar HaKappar teaches,
Life is transient; death no less so.[42]
The living are judged in order to know,
to understand, and to become aware of
God,
the Fashioner, Creator, Discerner,
Judge, Witness, and Plaintiff.[43]

The Blessed Holy One will judge.
Before God there is no iniquity,
forgetfulness, bias, or bribery.[44]
All that happens, happens as it must.[45]
Do not imagine that the grave brings
 peace.[46]
Despite your wishes you were
 conceived,
despite your wishes you were born,
despite your wishes you live,
despite your wishes you die,
despite your wishes you give an
 accounting before God,
the Blessed Holy One.[47]

**1** People are unique but not different. What makes you happy may not make another happy, but happiness itself is the same. Observe the behavior of others and learn what brings harmony and what brings discord.

**2** Psalm 119:99.

**3** The self cannot subdue itself, for the self that is subdued is only a projection of the self doing the subduing. This is only the spiritual cleverness of narrow mind. Rather, see that "you" can do nothing. When this is known, narrow mind naturally and effortlessly opens to spacious mind, and then there is nothing to do.

**4** Proverbs 16:32.

**5** Wealth is based not on what you can hold, but on what you can receive. Loving what is, you receive all that is, and rejoice; loving only what you want, you still receive all that is, but recoil.

**6** Psalm 128:2.

**7** Just as a cube of sugar sweetens a whole cup of tea, so honoring the One honors all, and honoring all honors the One; there is no separation between the two.

**8** 1 Samuel 2:30.

**9** Action generates action; wishing generates only frustration. Each act sets the conditions for the next. While you cannot control the results of your actions, you can influence the conditions they produce. The reward for kindness is the opportunity to do more kindness; the reward for cruelty is another opportunity to be cruel. Like dominoes falling one to the other, your actions become habits triggering more of the same. But unlike dominoes, you have the capacity to turn, to change, to be different in this moment. Abdicate that power and you abdicate your humanity.

**10** To scorn and mock imagines that persons and things can be extraneous or random, but this is not so. All that is at this moment is a result of the conditions that produce it. What is *is* because it must be. To scorn and mock is to deny the validity of what is, and this is a sign of great ignorance. Whatever exists in this hour has found its hour. Whatever exists in this place has found its place. Do not scorn what is, but embrace what is, no matter how painful. For without embracing what is, you cannot influence what is to come.

**11** Humility arises naturally from wisdom. Know what is, and humility is your response to what is. Does God have a plan for your life? Yes! To be a feast for worms. Knowing this frees you from narrow mind's addiction to immortality and allows you to be simply present in this moment.

**12** The Name is Reality, the Y-H-V-H that is what is. Desecrating the Name is living without attention, needlessly stirring suffering of self and other. There is no public and private in God, there is only the One. Just as a splash made "here" will ripple "there," so every private act has public consequences.

**13** Teaching Torah is sharing the menu; practicing Torah is sharing the meal. The one fills the mind; the other fills the belly. If you study in order to teach, your life is secondhand. If you study in order to practice, your life is firsthand, immediate. When you live in the immediacy of life, you find the means to study, teach, practice, and also to observe: to step back from the fleeting and see the eternal at its core.

**14** Narrow mind trusts in power and personal gain, and as such hoards them. Hoarding makes you fearful of losing, and fear of loss leads to fear of other. It is this that drives you out of the world.

**15** You honor Torah by embodying Her Wisdom. You embody Her Wisdom by respecting others. You respect others by engaging them with justice, compassion, and humility. Anything less is a disgrace to you and to Torah.

**16** Hated by those whom she judges, robbed of peace of mind by the demands of rendering decisions, lied to by those who seek to manipulate the outcome, a judge leads a life that is not to be envied.

**17** Those who judge in haste have no concern with truth and simply enforce their own opinion.

**18** If you are called to judge, seek counsel from others, for there are always facts and nuances that may escape you.

**19** If you judge with others and they do not agree with you, do not insist they yield, but trust in the wisdom of the majority.

**20** Do not allow the conditions of your life to determine the quality of your living. Those who can be just, kind, humble, and wise when poor will be so when rich. But those who reject these when rich will not live them when poor.

**21** Both work and study are part of life, but not equally so. Work can expand and leave you no time to deepen your wisdom. Set a limit on your work, and make time for study.

**22** Work pits you against another; study allies you with the other. Friendship and community are the rewards of Torah.

**23** Kindness protects you from the fear of the other, opening narrow mind to the greater unity of spacious mind. Cruelty feeds the fear of the other, forcing narrow mind to survive on its own. Turning to your true nature as the image and likeness of God makes kindness natural and keeps you from the madness of living in opposition to the other.

**24** Aligning with heaven is acting godly: doing justly, loving mercy, walking humbly. Aligning against heaven is acting selfishly: doing cleverly, loving conditionally, walking arrogantly. Every effort to discern Truth will endure, even if Truth is not found. Every effort to further delusion will not endure, even if Truth is found.

**25** Learning is a holy enterprise, and all who participate in it—students, teachers, and colleagues—deserve the highest respect from one another. The sages root this honor in God, the supreme teacher who offers wisdom to all who would but dare receive it.

**26** A careless teaching, one rooted in sacred opinion rather than Truth, can lead to actions no less harmful than those done deliberately at another's expense. Make sure all you share is true and not merely long held.

**27** There are three ways to rise in society: through intellect, through piety, and through power. None will matter if your reputation is smeared. Better a good name than all the world's titles.

**28** Learning is a cooperative exercise: the teacher challenges the student, the student challenges the teacher, and colleagues challenge one another. The moment the challenges cease, opinion freezes into fact, and ideas become idols barricaded against Truth.

**29** Proverbs 3:5. It is too easy to mistake your will for God's Will, your beliefs for Reality's Truth. Test what you know against the knowing of others, and test both against the unyielding simplicity of life.

**30** Why are the wicked not hounded by their wickedness? Why are the just so often robbed of peace? Do not settle for easy answers or abandon the questions themselves. Asking keeps you aware of injustice, and this may lead you to improve the world even as the answers themselves continue to elude you.

**31** When greeting another there is a moment's hesitation: Is this friend or foe? Assume that there is no foe, greet the other with honor and kindness, and discover only a friend.

**32** The lion is brave, the fox merely clever. Better to draw near to courage and see what is rather than to cleverly mask the truth with your own projected fantasy.

**33** The World to Come is this world seen from the perspective of spacious mind. Yet narrow mind traps your attention, and you imagine it is something else. Look deeply into this "something else," and it will fade like a shadow beneath the noonday sun. This is how you prepare yourself for the feast of the World to Come. Why a feast? Because when seen from spacious mind, scarcity gives way to abundance, hoarding to sharing, competition to cooperation, and suddenly there is enough for all.

**34** Eternity is simply the projection of hours on end, and so you equate the World to Come with eternal life of a permanent self. How boring—"you" dragging on forever! Turn to the true self now, and kindness defines your every act, and you will step out of time and the self that is its twin and awake to the One who is you now.

**35** Ecstasy is stepping out of narrow mind into spacious mind, out of time and into the Present. Without time there is no "I," no "you," no "self," no "other," for all these are a product of time and memory. Without them there is only God; within them, too, there is only God. That is why this world and the World to Come are the same world.

**36** Each moment has its purpose and right response. You tend to rush into change that is suiting what you want, without first allowing what is to play itself out. Nothing happens by accident. What is *is* because the conditions allow for it to be none other. You cannot change what is, but only the conditions that will determine what is next. You cannot change these conditions until the reality of the moment is allowed to play itself out. So let anger first rage before seeking to cool it. Let the bereaved bury their dead before burying their grief. Let one honor a vow before questioning its value. Let the burning pass before trying to ease one's shame.

**37** Shmuel is quoting Proverbs 24:17–18. What you do in this moment creates the condition for what you will experience in the next. If you take joy in another's pain, your arrogance will blind you, and you invite your own downfall. God doesn't punish you, but God doesn't spare you the punishments you set for yourself.

**38** Rabbi Elisha ben Avuya values the learning of the young over that of the old, for theirs is fresh and unsullied by changing opinions and misguided philosophies. But...

**39** Rabbi Yose values the learning of the old over that of the young, for the wisdom of youth is untested and without experience. But...

**40** Rabbi Meir reminds us that wisdom isn't the product of age but of insight. Youth does not make one wise, nor does old age make one foolish. Rather than look to the age of the teacher, gauge the quality of what she has to say.

**41** Narrow mind is not of the world, for it sees the world as other, as alien, something to conquer and defeat. Such a mind is driven by want and is forever at a loss to satisfy its ceaseless hunger. Hence jealousy, lust, and the desire for fame are the hallmarks of narrow mind. Spacious mind is of the world, for it sees the world and itself as part of the greater reality of God. Spacious mind does not want, for there is no lack when all is One. Hence jealously yields to compassion, lust yields to love, and fame is of no significance at all.

**42** Life and death are both tied to time in the world of narrow mind. Yet when you die, narrow mind opens to spacious mind, and you realize that the "you" you imagined yourself to be is a wave on the ocean that is God. As you die, you awake to the oceanic reality of your true self. The false self, the wave self, dies; the true self, the oceanic self, is unborn and undying.

**43** The grand drama of your life has but one actor—God. God is Friend and Foe, Beloved and Benighted, Self and Other. Know this and play hard, play well, and no one will get hurt.

**44** If God is all, then God is the bribed and the briber, the robbed and the robber. The drama of your life is the play of God.

**45** Everything arises from the conditions that are present at the moment of its arising and cannot be contrary to them. This is not fate or predestination; this is simply the nature of reality: snow melts, fire burns, an acorn cannot become other than an oak, and God cannot be other than reality. To want things to be other than they are, do not seek to change the things themselves, but to change the conditions that produced them.

**46** Peace is not the ending of conflict. Peace is the embracing of conflict without fear.

**47** Your wishes are powerless. The thought does not count. Reality is reality. You are born, live, and die because the conditions for your birth, life, and death require it. Intention is powerless unless it leads to action, and action is powerless unless it changes conditions. This is the accounting you must give before God: did you engage the conditions or did you wallow in your own delusion?

# Chapter Five

**5:1**
Why was the world created with ten sayings
when one would have sufficed?[1]
The ten refer to the ten punishments awaiting those who destroy the world,
and the ten rewards awaiting those who sustain it.[2]

**5:2**
Why were there ten generations from Adam to Noah?
To demonstrate God's patience, for each generation angered God,
but it took the cumulative disappointment of all ten to bring on the Flood.[3]

**5:3**
Why were there ten generations from Noah to Abraham?
To show God's patience, for each generation disappointed God,
but the tenth produced Abraham to receive the reward the others shunned.[4]

5:4
Why did Abraham endure ten trials?[5]
To demonstrate his love for God.[6]

5:5
Ten miracles were performed for our
 ancestors in Egypt,[7]
and ten at the Red Sea.
Ten plagues did God bring upon the
 Egyptians
in Egypt,
and ten more at the Sea.[8]

5:6
Ten times in the wilderness did our
 ancestors test
the Blessed Holy One:[9]
"They have tested Me these ten times
and did not heed My voice."[10]

5:7
Ten miracles were performed for our
 ancestors in the Holy Temple:
the stench of the sacrifice caused no
 miscarriages;
the sacrificial meat never spoiled;
the butchered flesh attracted no flies;

the High Priest was never unclean on Yom Kippur;
the sacrificial fires survived even the heaviest rain;
the barley offering of the *Omer*,[11]
the two loaves offering for Shavuot,[12]
and the showbread[13]
were always without blemish;[14]
the crowds, though massive,
always found room for prostrations;[15]
no serpent or scorpion struck inside Jerusalem; and
Jerusalem inns never lacked vacancies for pilgrims.

5:8
Ten things were created on the twilight of Sabbath:
the mouth of the earth;[16]
the mouth of the well;[17]
the mouth of the donkey;[18]
the rainbow;[19]
the manna;[20]
the staff;[21]

the *shamir*;[22]
the Hebrew alphabet;[23]

the stone inscriber;[24]
and the Tablets.[25]
Some say also destructive spirits,[26]
Moses's grave,[27]
the ram that replaced Isaac on Abraham's altar,[28]
and the tongs that are made with tongs.[29]

5:9
Seven traits characterize a fool and seven a sage.
A sage
keeps silent before wisdom and age;
does not interrupt the words of another;
is slow to answer;[30]
questions insightfully,[31] and replies concisely;[32]
prioritizes matters in order of importance;[33]
admits to what is not known;[34] and accepts correction graciously.[35]
The fool does the opposite of these.

5:10
Seven errors bring seven punishments.

If some are generous and others are
 not, the rain ceases,
famine comes, and some will eat while
 others starve.
If none are generous, drought and
 bandits rob the land of food
and all go hungry.
If the people fail to give thanks for
 their bounty,
drought and famine are the result.[36]

5:11
If the courts are weak,
or if fruits of the Sabbatical year are
 not left to the poor,
pestilence is the result.
If justice is delayed or perverted,
or if Torah is used to excuse
 unrighteousness,
the sword of war comes to the world.
Vain oaths and desecration of God's
 Name bring on wild beasts.
Idolatry, immorality, murder,
and refusal to let the earth rest during
 the Sabbatical year
cause exile from the land.[37]

5:12

Four periods during the seven-year
 Sabbatical cycle
are most prone to plague:
the fourth, the seventh, the first of the
 new cycle,
and each fall after the festival of
 Sukkot.
Why the fourth year?
Because people neglect to collect for
 the poor in the third year.
Why the seventh?
Because people neglect to collect for
 the poor in the sixth year.
Why the first year of a new cycle?
Because people did not leave the
 produce of the
Sabbatical year.
And why after Sukkot?
Because people rob the poor of their
 gifts.[38]

5:13
People fall into four types:
Those who say,
"What's mine is mine, and what's yours
 is yours";
this is the average, though some say
 this is the type predominant in Sodom.
Those who say,

"What's mine is yours, and what's yours is mine as well";
this is the fool.
Those who say,
"What's mine is yours, and what's yours is yours";
this is the saint.
Those who say,
"What is mine is mine, and what's yours is mine";
this is the wicked.[39]

5:14
People fall into four temperaments:
Those who anger quickly and pacify just as quickly;
their loss is balanced by their gain.
Those who anger slowly and pacify just as slowly;
their gain is balanced by their loss.
Those who anger slowly and pacify quickly;
they are the pious.
Those who anger quickly and pacify slowly;
they are the wicked.[40]

5:15
New students fall into four categories:

Those who grasp quickly and forget just as quickly;
their gain is balanced by their loss.
Those who grasp slowly and forget slowly;
their loss is balanced by their gain.
Those who grasp quickly and forget slowly;
these are good students.
Those who grasp slowly and forget quickly;
these are poor students.[41]

5:16
Donors fall into four types:
Those who wish to give and wish others not give;
they rob others of merit.
Those who urge others to give but do not give themselves;
they rob themselves of merit.
Those who give and urge others to give;
they are the compassionate.
Those who do not give and urge others not to give;
these are the wicked.[42]

5:17

Longtime students fall into four
 categories:
Those who go to the House of Study
 but do not study;
these are rewarded for going.
Those who study at home but do not
 go to the House of Study;
these are rewarded for learning.
Those who go the House of Study and
 study;
these are rewarded for going and
 learning.
Those who neither go nor study; these
 are fools.[43]

5:18
Disciples fall into four categories:
Those who absorb everything, both what
 is true and what is not;
these are called sponges.
Those who take it all in and let it all
 out;
these are called funnels.
Those who take in the wine, but retain
 only the sediment;
these are called strainers.
Those who take in both wheat and
 chaff, but retain only the fine flour;
these are called sieves.[44]

5:19
Contingent love cannot outlast its cause.
Noncontingent love is timeless.[45]
The love of Amnon for Tamar—this is contingent love;
when Tamar's beauty fades, Amnon's love ceases.[46]
The love of David and Jonathan—this is noncontingent love;
even in competition their love never ceases.[47]

5:20
Conflict for the sake of Truth yields good results.
Conflict for the sake of power yields poison.[48]
The conflict between Hillel and Shammai—
this is for the sake of Truth.[49]
The conflict between Korach and his community—
this is for the sake of power.[50]

5:21
If you influence people toward goodness,
you need not fear the result.[51]

If you influence them toward violence,
you will not escape violence.⁵²
Moses influenced the people toward
 goodness,
and their merit was ascribed to him as
 well,
as it is said,
"He performed the righteousness of God,
and God's laws together with Israel."⁵³
Jeroboam ben Nebat sinned
and influenced the people to sin,
so their sin is added to his sin,
as it is said,
"For the sins of Jeroboam which he
 committed
and which he caused Israel to
 commit."⁵⁴

5:22
Three traits are found among the
 disciples of Abraham:
a good eye,
a humble spirit,
and a generous soul.⁵⁵
Three traits are found among the
 disciples of Balaam:
an evil eye,
an arrogant spirit,

and a greedy soul.⁵⁶
The disciples of Abraham enjoy this world
and inherit the World to Come,⁵⁷
as it is said,
"To cause those who love Me to inherit an everlasting possession,
and I will fill their storehouses."⁵⁸
The disciples of Balaam inherit Gehinnom
and descend into the well of destruction,⁵⁹
as it is said,
"And You, O God, shall lower them into the well of
destruction,
murderers and liars shall not live out half their days;
but as for me, I will trust in You."⁶⁰

5:23
Yehudah ben Tema teaches,
Be bold as a leopard,
light as an eagle,
swift as a deer,
and strong as a lion to carry out the will of your Father in heaven.⁶¹

**5:24**
Yehudah ben Tema used to teach,
Arrogance leads to Gehinnom, humility to the Garden of Eden.[62]
May it be Your will, *HaShem*, our God and God of our forefathers,
that the Holy Temple be rebuilt speedily in our days,
and grant us our share in Your Torah.[63]

**5:25**
Yehudah ben Tema used to teach,
At five years old begin to study the Bible,
at ten open the Mishnah.[64]
At thirteen take on the commandments,[65]
and at fifteen begin to study Gemara.[66]
Marry at eighteen,
and secure a career at twenty.
Full strength comes at thirty,
but understanding waits until forty.[67]
At fifty begin to counsel,
and at sixty take your place as an elder.[68]
Old age begins with seventy,
but at eighty you still have power.
At ninety you bend with age,

and at one hundred be as one dead,
passing beyond the cares of this world.[69]

5:26
Ben Bag Bag teaches,
Turn Her and turn Her for all things are
 in Her;
look deeply into Her,
grow old and gray over Her,
and do not depart from Her,
for there is nothing that surpasses Her.[70]

Ben Hei Hei teaches,
Effort is its own reward.[71]

**1** In the Hebrew Bible, the phrase "God said" is used ten times in Genesis 1:1–2:18. Jewishly, the number ten signifies wholeness, suggesting that creation is a unity-through-diversity. More importantly, Genesis is saying that creation as a whole is the Word of God, the way God incarnates in and as time and space.

**2** The sages do not list what these ten punishments and rewards are, suggesting a more metaphoric understanding: those who work to destroy the world, denying its unity and making idols of diversity, are destroyed by the world, while those who work to sustain the world, affirming both diversity and unity in a greater nonduality, are themselves sustained by the world.

**3** While each act has its immediate consequence, transformation is due to the accumulative effect of many actions over time. If one generation goes bad, the next can correct matters. If evil becomes a habit, destruction will inevitably result. Yet...

**4** Even a single generation can turn the tide of destruction if that generation is powerful and daring enough. Abraham broke with the conditioning of his culture, his tribe, and his family and changed the direction of human history (Genesis 12:1). True spiritual transformation comes not from imitating the past, but from breaking with it, and reconnecting with the eternal present that is God.

**5** The ten trials are leaving his home for the Land of Israel (Genesis 12:1); forced exile in Egypt because of famine (Genesis 12:10); Sarah's abduction by Pharaoh (Genesis 12:15); the battle with the four kings (Genesis 14); taking Hagar as his concubine (Genesis 16:1–3); circumcision in his old age (Genesis 17); Sarah's abduction by Avimelech (Genesis 20:2); the expulsion of Hagar and Ishmael from his home (Genesis 21:9–14); the binding and near-sacrifice of Isaac on Mount Moriah (Genesis 22:1–19); and the purchase of a burial plot for Sarah (Genesis 23).

**6** Love for God translates as a passion for life lived with wisdom, justice, compassion, and humility. Living this love means facing life's challenges with that love, and this Abraham did ten times, allowing each to strengthen his resolve to meet the next with the same love.

**7** What were miracles for the Hebrews were plagues for the Egyptians: water to blood (Exodus 7:19), frogs (Exodus 8:2), gnats (Exodus 8:12), flies (Exodus 8:20), mad cow disease (Exodus 9:3), boils (Exodus 9:9), hail (Exodus 9:18), locusts (Exodus 10:4), darkness (Exodus 10:21), death of the firstborn (Exodus 11:5). The label doesn't matter, what matters is the result. The actions in Egypt and at the Sea promoted freedom, and for those who desired freedom, they were miracles; for those committed to slavery, they were plagues.

**8** There is no biblical basis for the claim that ten additional plagues and miracles happened at the Sea. This is more poetic license on the part of the sages than scriptural reference.

**9** God's word is the world. To ignore God's voice is to act contrary to the laws of nature, both physical and moral. While you are free to try, the result is always the same: failure. While you cannot control the current of life, you can learn to work with it to bring justice and joy to self and other.

**10** Numbers 14:22. While the number ten is used, there is no actual list of the ten tests.

**11** The *Omer* is a sheaf of barley offered in the Temple on the morning of the sixteenth of Nisan to mark the season when people could eat the new grain crop. See Leviticus 23:19.

**12** Shavuot is the anniversary of the giving of the Ten Commandments on Mount Sinai. The two loaves remind us of the two tablets upon which the Ten Commandments were inscribed. See Leviticus 23:17.

**13** Showbread are the twelve loaves baked each Friday and placed on the altar in the Temple on the Sabbath. See Exodus 25:30 and Leviticus 24:5.

**14** These miracles defy the laws of probability. The Rabbis are saying that the work of the Temple was of an order outside the normal contingencies of nature.

**15** When you actualize your uniqueness in the greater unity of God, you find there is room for everyone. When you ignore your uniqueness and imitate others, the world suddenly has no room or need for you at all.

**16** The earthquake that swallowed Korach and his rebels after their failed rebellion against Moses and Aaron (Numbers 16:32).

**17** Miriam, the older sister of both Moses and his brother, Aaron, was the first woman to be called a prophet (Exodus 15:20). According to Jewish legend it was Miriam's righteousness that caused a well to follow the

Hebrews through their wanderings in the desert. When she died, the well disappeared, some saying it was hidden in the Sea of Galilee. The legend's origins are in the juxtaposition of texts in the Torah: Miriam dies in Numbers 20:1 and the people suddenly are without water in 20:2. The proximity of these two texts led to the notion that the first caused the second, and to the legend of Miriam's well. (See Rashi on Numbers 20:2; *Taanit* 9a; Song of Songs Rabbah 4:14, 27).

**18** The donkey that spoke to Balaam (Numbers 22:28). Balaam was a magician hired by the Moabite king Balak to curse the Israelites. On his way to do so, God sent an angel to block his path, but only his donkey could see it. Unaware of the angel, Balaam kept urging his donkey to go forward. The frustrated animal miraculously spoke to Balaam, revealing the angel's presence and leading him to bless the Israelites instead of curse them. His blessing (*Mah tovu*/How goodly are your tents, O Jacob

[Numbers 24:5]) is a regular part of the Jewish liturgy.

**19** The rainbow that signaled God's covenant with life (Genesis 9:17) and God's promise never again to destroy the earth with water.

**20** The food God supplied to the Israelites during their forty years of wandering in the desert (Exodus 16:31). Manna was said to have no taste of its own, but to take on the flavor of any kosher food one desired.

**21** The staff Moses used to perform miracles in Egypt (Exodus 4:17). According to rabbinic tradition the staff belonged to Adam and was inscribed with the four-letter Name of God, Y-H-V-H.

**22** To signify it as a house of peace, the stones of Solomon's Temple were not to be cut by blades that could be used as weapons (Exodus 20:22). Rabbinic tradition says God provided the builders with a worm, called *shamir,* that split large stones as it crawled over them.

**23** Hebrew is the language God spoke to bring the world into being. The letters of the Hebrew alphabet are doorways to the heart of creation.

**24** The tool God used to write the first set of tablets (Exodus 32:15). Some say this was the *shamir* later used to cut the stones for Solomon's Temple.

**25** The tablets upon which the Ten Commandments were inscribed (Exodus 32:16).

**26** These are the ideas that foster the delusion of the separate and sovereign self.

**27** No one knows where Moses is buried, to avoid making it and him into an object of worship (Deuteronomy 34:6).

**28** The Binding of Isaac is an evolutionary turning point in human spirituality, marking the shift from human sacrifice to animal sacrifice (Genesis 22:13). It will take centuries for the prophets to effect another turning, shifting human spirituality from sacrifice of others to sacrifice of self and selfishness.

**29** Tongs are made by heating metal until it is red-hot. To spare the hands of the smith, the heated metal must be held with another set of tongs. The Rabbis imagined that God provided humans with the first set of tongs, thus allowing them to make subsequent sets. Taken metaphorically, we are taught that before you can make something, you have to imagine the possibility of its existence. Imagination, then, is the first and most powerful tool of all.

**30** Again you are reminded that silence is key to wisdom. One should cultivate silence in order to honor one who exceeds you in wisdom and in years, to listen to another's wisdom, to consider your answers that you reply not simply to the question posed but to the concern that hides behind it.

**31** Questioning is the master tool of wisdom: ask the right question and you will find the truth.

**32** Too many words suggest too little wisdom; Truth is complex, but never complicated.

**33** Know what matters and deal with it. Leave the rest alone.

**34** The wise know that they do not know. This is what makes them wise.

**35** The sage is not averse to correction, for she is never afraid of learning.

**36** Humans are *adam,* "earthlings," and our actions have consequences on our home, *adamah,* "earth." Do not imagine that what you do affects you alone. There is no "you alone"; there is only you in the All One.

**37** Social justice is essential to human survival. If the law does not protect people from predators, or the earth from exploitation and over-cultivation; if the law is used to pervert justice, or if courts fail to adhere to the standards of law in trials; then society crumbles and the people are exiled, having forfeited their right to their homes. There is no right free from responsibility. You reap what you sow.

**38** Here, too, justice for the poor and powerless determines the quality of a society and is a barometer of its destiny. The Sabbatical year is to be a year of rest for the earth, allowing her to rejuvenate. The foods that grow during this period are not to be used by the owners of the land, but are to be left for the poor. Similarly, at the fall Sukkot harvest, gleanings and what grows in the corners of the field are to be left for the poor and landless. When this isn't done, greed overwhelms the world and all suffer.

**39** Ownership is a delusion of narrow mind. All you have is yours on loan, a temporary gift providing temporary benefit. You can measure a person's level of insight into this fact by her or his level of attachment to possessions. The more attachment, the less wisdom.

You may think, however, that the saint becomes a drain on the community, giving up all she has to others. But the "you" the saint acknowledges as the true owner of things is not the other, but God: What's mine is Yours, and what's Yours is Yours, for it is all You.

**40** If lack of greed is a measure of the wise mind, lack of anger is the measure of the wise heart. Anger arises from fear, and fear is rooted in the delusion of your separateness from others and from God. The wise know they are not the target, for there is no self or other with whom to contest.

**41** A supple mind and a strong memory are the measure of good students.

**42** Just as greed is the hallmark of the wicked, so too stinginess. Narrow mind operates in a world of scarcity. There is never enough food, water, wealth, possessions, honor, justice, power, or fame. So narrow mind needs to grasp all it can and hoard all it has. Yet the fear that drives narrow mind is challenged by the openhearted fearlessness of generosity. So it is not enough that you hoard and refuse to share it with the poor; you must make sure others hoard as well and in this way protect the fearful lifestyle you have chosen.

**43** Learning is a lifelong commitment, but over time you may find that commitment lagging. You may take a class but be so filled with past knowledge you have no room for new ideas. You may study at home and review what you already know but be wary of learning something new from someone else. You may avoid learning altogether and thus fall into the trap of ignorance. The only way to become wise is to test what you know against what you do not know in a community of learners doing the same.

**44** A student pursues knowledge; a disciple is in quest of wisdom. There are those who cannot distinguish between what is wise and what is merely clever; these are filled with both but become neither. There are those who sit in awe of the sage and don't retain a word of wisdom, mistaking the messenger for the message. There are those who see both wisdom and cleverness but mistake the one for the other and retain nothing of value. The true disciple is one who can discern the true from the merely clever, retaining the former and dropping the latter.

**45** Love that depends upon something outside itself will die when that something is gone. You see this all the time. Love dependent on youth dies with age. Love dependent on beauty fades when beauty fades. Love dependent on wealth ends when wealth disappears. But love that is rooted not in externals but in the very being of the beloved, this love lasts even after the beloved has died.

**46** Amnon loved Tamar for her beauty (2 Samuel 13).

**47** David and Jonathan loved each other for who they were. Even in competition for the throne of Israel, their love did not cease (1 Samuel 18).

**48** Conflict in and of itself is not bad. What matters is the goal toward which the conflict aims. When you struggle with others to uncover Truth, the struggle is for the good. When you struggle with others to enhance your position and weaken theirs, the conflict will poison you and all you do.

**49** Hillel and Shammai took opposite sides on most issues of rabbinic concern, yet they did so not to weaken each other, but to strengthen the quest for truth.

**50** Korach and his rebels sought power for themselves at the expense of Moses (Numbers 16:1–3).

**51** Your actions are under your control, but not so the results of your actions. The best intentions can lead to unexpected and unwanted results. Yet this should not excuse passivity and inaction. The sage acts in the service of justice and compassion, and trusts that whatever the results, justice and compassion will be enhanced, even if not in the manner intended. Act rightly and well and for the right reason, and know you have done all you can.

**52** If you act for power, your actions will be tinged with violence and incite violence in others. This will bring you further violence, pain, and suffering.

**53** Deuteronomy 33:21.

**54** 1 Kings 15:30.

**55** Disciples of Abraham do what Abraham did: free themselves from the conditioning of nation, tribe, culture, religion, and family to see the world as God sees it—precious, sacred, and whole (Genesis 12:1). Hence they cultivate a good eye that sees the interdependence of life and the transcendent unity that embraces it, a humble spirit that seeks to serve the whole rather than control it, and a generous soul rooted in the abundance of God's grace rather than in the scarcity of personal power.

**56** Disciples of Balaam do what Balaam did: seek to curse those who reveal the unity of life in God and the universal justice and compassion that arise from it (Numbers 22–23). Hence they cultivate an evil eye that separates and divides, an arrogant spirit that seeks to control rather than cooperate, and a greedy soul that hoards its power rather than spreads its wealth.

**57** Disciples of Abraham see this world as the World to Come, knowing that each is a manifestation of the One who is God.

**58** Proverbs 8:21.

**59** Disciples of Balaam live in fear because they rule through fear. Fear itself is Gehinnom, hell, the well of destruction that robs you of joy, companionship, trust, and faith.

**60** Psalm 55:24.

**61** The will of God is the working of reality here and now. At each moment reality presents you with something that needs doing. Do it unhesitatingly, with grace, attention, and courage. This is the reason you were born.

**62** Arrogance masks fear, and fear is hell. Humility is the face that needs no mask, and this itself is heaven.

**63** The Temple is the living link between the Whole and the parts. In ancient times the people needed a physical place to remember this link. May it come to pass that we realize that we ourselves are the Temple in which the part and Whole are made one. In this way we are granted our share of Torah, becoming living examples of the Divine Teaching.

**64** The Mishnah is the Oral Torah said to be given by God to Moses and passed on verbally from teacher to disciple until the time of Yehudah HaNasi, who had it committed to writing in the third century CE.

**65** Thirteen is the age Abraham is said to have been when he shattered the idols of his father and took on the yoke of obedience to the One God. Here, too, we are to break with the idols of self and selfishness and yoke ourselves to the service of God and godliness.

**66** Gemara is commentary on the Mishnah. Together, Mishnah and Gemara compose the Talmud. The Gemara was written down in the sixth century CE.

**67** Understanding is not abstract, but rooted in long experience with family and work.

**68** As your understanding grows, you share what you have learned, but it isn't until this counsel is tested over time that you are ready to call yourself an elder. Age alone means nothing. Age deepened by experience is the key.

**69** At ninety the weight of the world takes its toll, and you bend under its burden. It is time to let it go so that at one hundred you have neither cares nor desires, and hence are as one dead to the hungers and fears of temporal life.

**70** Though later understood to refer to Torah, the "Her" here is Wisdom, the way of life unfolding in the greater unity of God. Examine each moment and its call; look deeply into what is that you might move in harmony with it; do not imagine you are apart from Her, for there is nothing that is other in the One Who Is God.

**71** The reward for your effort is the effort itself. Do not imagine that you will earn something at the end of your life; your life itself is the gift. There is no point to living; living is the point. There is no purpose to living; living is the purpose. As long as you imagine that doing leads to getting, you will never appreciate the act of doing.

# Chapter Six

The sages taught in the language of the Mishnah.
Blessed is the One who chose them and their teachings.[1]

6:1
Rabbi Meir teaches,
Those who study Torah for Her own sake merit many things.[2]
The entire world is counted worthy for their sake.[3]
They are called Friend and Beloved.
They love and gladden God and creation.
They are clothed in humility and wonder.
They are righteous, devout, fair, and faithful.
They are drawn from sin toward merit.
They provide counsel and wisdom, understanding and strength,[4]
as it is said,
"Mine are counsel and wisdom, I am understanding, Mine is strength."[5]

They lead and rule, and reason
 critically.
Torah's secrets are known to them.[6]
They are fountains that never weaken,
rivers that never dry out.
They are humble, patient, and forgiving
 of insults.
They are great and rise above all
 things.[7]

6:2
Rabbi Yehoshua ben Levi teaches,
Every day the Daughter's Voice[8] echoes
 from Mount Horeb,[9] saying,
"Woe to those who insult Torah!"
Whoever ignores Torah is called
 "Rebuked,"[10]
as it is said,
"Like a gold ring in a pig's nose
is a beautiful woman who abandons
 reason."[11]
And it says,
"The Tablets are God's handiwork, and
 the script is
God's script engraved on the Tablets."[12]
Do not read "engraved" [charut] but
 "freedom" [cherut],

for there is no freedom outside of Torah.
And all who study Torah are elevated, as it is said,
"From *Mattanah* to *Nachaliel,* and from *Nachaliel* to *Bamot.*"[13]

6:3
Honor every teacher whether they teach you a single chapter,
a single law, a single verse, a single saying, or even a single letter.[14]
This we learn from David, who learned but two things from Achitophel
yet called him his teacher, his guide, and his intimate:
"You are the man of my measure, my guide, and my intimate."[15]
If David, King of Israel, so honors Achitophel,
one who learns a single chapter, a single law, a single verse,
a single saying, even a single letter from another
must honor that other even more.
Yet honor belongs not only to the teacher but to Torah as well,[16]
as it is said,

"The wise shall inherit honor"[17] and
"the just shall inherit goodness."[18]
Only Torah is good,
as it is said,
"I have given you a good teaching, do not forsake My Torah."[19]

6:4
This is the way of Torah:
Eat bread with salt;
drink enough water;[20]
sleep on the ground;[21]
live a life of simplicity;[22]
and toil in Torah.[23]
If you do this, "You are praiseworthy, and all is well with you."[24]
You are praiseworthy in this world, and all will be well in the World to Come.[25]

6:5
Do not seek greatness nor crave honor;
let your service exceed your learning.
Do not lust for the table of kings,
For your feast is the greater, as is your crown,[26]

and your Employer can be trusted to pay you for your efforts.[27]

6:6
Torah surpasses priesthood and royalty. Royalty carries thirty benefits and priesthood twenty-four,[28] but Torah bestows forty-eight benefits on the wise:
time to study, the capacity to listen with attention,
and speak with clarity;
understanding, intuition, awe, reverence, modesty, joy, and purity;
serving teachers, befriending colleagues, and debating students;
deliberation, and knowledge of Scripture and Mishnah;
fewer complications from business, sex, pleasure,
exhaustion, small talk, and silliness;
patience, compassion, trust, equanimity, belonging, acceptance, and privacy;
humility, feeling loved, and loving God, creation, goodness, justice, and guidance;
avoiding honors, humble in learning, and free from literalism;

sharing another's burden, judging others favorably,
setting people on the true path, and the path of peace;
thinking freely, asking boldly and answering truthfully,
listening and sharing, learning and teaching, and learning and practicing;
enhancing the wisdom of your teacher, pondering over what you learn, and giving honor to another by sharing their teaching in their name,[29]
for whoever repeats a teaching in the teacher's name
brings redemption to the world,
as it is said,
"And Esther said to the king in the name of Mordechai."[30]

6:7
Great is Torah, for it confers life upon its practitioners
both in this world and the World to Come,[31]
as it is said,
"For they are life to those who find them,
and a healing to their entire flesh."[32]

And it says,
"It shall be healing to your body,
and marrow to your bones."[33]
And it says,
"It is a tree of life to those who grasp it,
and its supporters are praiseworthy."[34]
And it says,
"They are a garland of grace for your head,
and necklaces for your neck."[35]
And it says,
"It will give to your head a garland of grace,
a crown of glory it will deliver to you."[36]
And it says,
"Indeed, through me your days shall be increased,
and years of life shall be added to you."[37]
And it says,
"Lengthy days are at its right
and at its left are wealth and honor."[38]
And it says,
"For lengthy days and years of life,
and peace shall they add to you."[39]

6:8

Rabbi Shimon ben Yehudah teaches in the name of Rabbi Shimon ben Yochai,
Beauty, strength, wealth, honor, wisdom,
old age, hoary age, and children—
these befit the righteous and the world,[40]
as it is said,
"Ripe old age is a crown of splendor; it can be found in the path of righteousness."[41]
And it says,
"The crown of the aged is grandchildren, and the splendor of children is their parents."[42]
And it says,
"The splendor of young men is their strength,
and the glory of old men is hoary age."[43]
And it says,
"The moon will grow pale and the sun be shamed,
when *HaShem*, Master of Legions,
will have reigned on Mount Zion and in Jerusalem,

and honor shall be before God's
 elders."⁴⁴

Rabbi Shimon ben Menasya said,
These seven qualities that the sages
 attribute to the righteous
were realized in Rabbi and his sons.⁴⁵

6:9
Rabbi Yose ben Kisma teaches,
Once I was walking on the road, when
 a certain man met me.
He greeted me and I returned the
 greeting.
He said to me, Rabbi, where are you
 from?
I told him I was from a city famous for
 its scholars and sages.
He said to me, Rabbi, I would pay you
 millions in gold,
precious stones, and pearls
if you would live with us in our place.
I replied, Even if you were to offer all
 the wealth in the world,
still I would not reside in a place empty
 of Torah.⁴⁶
And so it is written, "I prefer the Torah
 of Your mouth

over thousands in gold and silver."[47]
Furthermore, when a person departs
 from this world,
only Torah and kindness accompany
 him,[48]
while silver, gold, precious stones, and
 pearls stay behind.
As it is said,
"When you walk, it shall guide you;
when you lie down, it shall guard you;
and when you awake, it shall speak on
 your behalf."[49]
"When you walk"—in this world;
"when you lie down it shall guard
 you"—in the grave;
"and when you awake, it shall speak
 on your behalf"—in the World to Come.
And it says,
Mine is the silver, and Mine is the gold,
says *HaShem*, Master of Legions.[50]

6:10
Five possessions did the Blessed Holy
 One acquire in the world:
Torah, heaven and earth, Abraham,
 Israel, and the Holy Temple.[51]

About Torah it is written,

"*HaShem* created me at the beginning of the divine unfolding,
the first of God's ancient works."[52]

About heaven and earth it is written,
"The heaven is My throne, and the earth is My footstool;
what House can you build for Me, and where is the place of My rest?"[53]
And it says,
"How abundant are Your works, *HaShem*,
with wisdom You made them all, the earth is full of Your possessions."[54]

About Abraham it is written,
"And God blessed him and said: Blessed is Abram of God the Most High,
Who acquired heaven and earth."[55]

About Israel is it written,
"Until Your people passes through, *HaShem*, until it passes through—
this people You acquired."[56]
And it also says,
"But for the holy ones who are in the earth

and for the mighty all my desires are due to them."[57]

About the Holy Temple it is written,
"Your dwelling-place that You, *HaShem*, have made;
the Sanctuary, that Your hands established."[58]
And it says, "And God brought them to the sacred boundary,
to this mountain which God's right hand acquired."[59]

6:11
All that the Blessed Holy One created in the world,
God created solely for God's glory,[60]
as it is said,
"All that is called by My Name, indeed, it is for My glory that I have created it,
formed it, and made it."[61]
And it says,
"God shall reign for all eternity."[62]

**1** Originally *Pirke Avot* ended with chapter five. Since the Mishnah, of which *Pirke Avot* is a part, contains six sections, a sixth section was added to *Pirke Avot.* The teachings in this section are called *beraytot,* literally teachings preserved from "outside" the Mishnah that are written in the style of the Mishnah.

**2** *Torah lishmah,* studying Torah for Her own sake, is the process of emptying your egoistic self that you might receive the Wisdom that is Torah.

**3** The purpose of creation is to evolve a level of consciousness that sees God manifest in and as all things. *Torah lishmah* awakens this awareness.

**4** These epithets tell us the role of the sage. The sage is God's friend and beloved, one who knows the world as God's manifestation, and thereby brings joy to God and creation by engaging all beings justly and with compassion.

**5** Proverbs 8:14. Realizing yourself as God, you become a vehicle for God's counsel, wisdom, understanding, and strength.

**6** The secrets of Torah are three: the secret of self—you are the image and likeness of God (Genesis 1:26); the secret of other—God is all that is (Exodus 3:14); the secret of right living—do justly, love mercy, walk humbly (Micah 6:8).

**7** To rise above all things is to be free from the anxiety that accompanies attachment to the temporal and finite, rather than seeing them as expressions of the timeless and infinite.

**8** The sages experienced revelation as *Bat Kol,* literally the "Voice of the Daughter." Who is the Daughter? *Chochmah,* "Wisdom," God's firstborn (Proverbs 8:22).

**9** Mount Horeb is another name for Mount Sinai.

**10** How do you insult Torah? By taking Her literally. A literal reading reduces Her to one place and one time. Reading Torah as metaphor and myth frees Her to speak to you in your place and your time. How do you ignore Torah? By focusing only on what She says and not what She means.

**11** Proverbs 11:22. A woman who relies on beauty alone will find herself attached to one who is more pig than partner. A woman's reason, not her beauty, is her true treasure.

**12** Exodus 32:16. The wordplay demonstrates the playful, creative nature of *Torah lishmah.* The Hebrew Bible is written without vowels, allowing the reader to discover different words and multiple meanings in the text by reading in different vowels. Rather than read the literal *charut,* "engraved," they read *cherut,* "freedom," revealing that true freedom comes from the pursuit of wisdom.

**13** Numbers 21:19. Again the Rabbis play with Torah, this time by reading place names as nouns. *Mattanah* means "gift," *Nachaliel* means "divine heritage," and *Bamot* means "high places." The gift of Torah leads to reclaiming your divine heritage as the image and likeness of God, which lifts you up beyond the drama of narrow mind to the peace of spacious mind.

**14** You receive only in order to transmit, and you must seek to share what you know, even if you know very little. Similarly, no matter how much or how little you learn from another, you owe that other your deepest respect, for your life would not be as rich were it not for their teaching. The Jewish tradition of citing the name of the teacher from whom you learned what it is you are teaching is demonstrated throughout *Pirke Avot*.

**15** Psalm 55:14. Tradition says Achitophel taught David to study with a friend and to walk joyously when going to the House of God.

**16** To protect the teacher from imagining that the merit due them is due to them, the sages remind you that honor comes from what is taught and not the one who teaches it.

**17** Proverbs 3:35. Honor is not sought, but comes of its own when wisdom is cultivated.

**18** Proverbs 28:10. Goodness is not sought, but comes of its own when justice is cultivated.

**19** Proverbs 4:2. To forsake Torah is to forsake the teaching it contains: One God manifest as one creation, realized by one humanity living by one moral code—justice and compassion for all.

**20** The way of Torah, the way to shift from narrow mind to spacious mind, is the way of simplicity but not asceticism. Hence you are to eat bread with salt, for these together were thought to be a complete meal, and drink enough water to maintain your health.

**21** This hints at Jacob, who slept on the ground in Haran and dreamed of the ladder linking heaven and earth (Genesis 28:12). Sleeping on the ground means cultivating dreams that reveal the unity of this world and the World to Come.

**22** A simple life in this context means a life not caught up in either busyness or business. Earn enough to be free of undue financial worry, but leave most of your time for study.

**23** To toil in Torah is to make time for study, to read Scripture in a way that reveals the secrets of God's nonduality and your place in the divine unfolding.

**24** Psalm 128:2.

**25** The sages place "praiseworthy" in this world and "all is well" in the World to Come. They know that all is not always well in this world, the world of seemingly competing selves dominated by narrow mind. But one who learns to live justly and kindly in this world, regardless of life's hardships, is called praiseworthy. One who sees through this world into the World to Come, who makes narrow mind a conduit for spacious mind and thus transforms fear into love, this one knows that all is as it is because it cannot be other than it is, and hence experiences life with a deep equanimity and peace. For such a person, all is well, for all is God.

**26** Again the sages use the image of the feast to describe the nature of this world when seen from the perspective of spacious mind. Scarcity and the fear that fosters it are anathema to God and God-realization. To lust for the table of kings is to mistake temporal power for timeless presence.

**27** This theme is reflected throughout our text: effort is rewarded, not the ends. Not everyone is a great sage, but everyone can seek wisdom. God does not measure the results; the effort is the reward.

**28** These are the benefits accrued by a life devoted to wisdom rather than piety or power. They fall into three broad categories: personal, interpersonal, and transpersonal.

Personally, a life of study provides you with freedom from worry. Interpersonally you have the opportunity to be of service to others as student, teacher, guide, and friend. Transpersonally, you cultivate the gifts of self-transcendence, allowing you to see the world from spacious mind and discover it to be none other than the World to Come.

**29** You honor your teachers by keeping their names alive through their teachings. Whenever you share what you have learned from another, take care to share also the name of the other from whom you learned it.

**30** Esther 2:22.

**31** Torah is not a book of law but a way of life rooted in the timeless principles of justice, compassion, and humility that arise when you reclaim your true name as the image and likeness of God. Applying these principles to the ever-changing contingencies of your life is the way of Torah.

**32** Proverbs 4:22.

**33** Proverbs 3:8.

**34** Proverbs 3:18.

**35** Proverbs 1:9.

**36** Proverbs 4:9.

**37** Proverbs 9:11.

**38** Proverbs 3:16.

**39** Proverbs 3:2.

**40** A sage's beauty?—the elegance of his teaching. A sage's strength?—the depth of her deeds. A sage's wealth?—the breadth of her knowledge. A sage's honor?—the love of his students. A sage's wisdom?—her knowledge of self. A sage's old age?—his willingness to grow. A sage's hoary age?—her capacity for the timeless. And a sage's children?—the teachings that outlive her.

**41** Proverbs 16:31.

**42** Proverbs 17:6.

**43** Proverbs 20:29.

**44** Isaiah 24:23. Isaiah 24:23.

**45** "Rabbi" is Yehudah HaNasi, Judah the Prince, who was the chief sage at the time the Mishnah was codified.

**46** A place empty of Torah is a place trapped in the worship of power and possessions, a place where narrow mind has no inkling of spacious mind, and where fear drives out love. Do not imagine that you can go to such a place and transform it by yourself. Wisdom arises from the community of sages, and no sage should see herself as self-sufficient.

**47** Psalm 119:72.

**48** When you depart this world and shift from narrow mind to spacious mind, your interest in wealth fades and your appreciation for wisdom grows.

**49** Proverbs 6:22.

**50** *Chagigah* 2:8.

**51** What most clearly reveals the presence of God? Torah: the teachings of God's prophets and sages. Heaven and earth: the timeless and the temporal. Abraham: the one who freed himself from conditionality to see the One as the many. Israel: those wounded healers who wrestle with life in service to God, walking at the pace of the nursing. The Holy Temple: the place where service to God and God Itself are realized as one.

**52** Proverbs 8:22.

**53** Isaiah 66:1.

**54** Psalm 104:24.

**55** Genesis 14:19.

**56** Exodus 15:16.

**57** Psalm 16:3.

**58** Exodus 15:17.

**59** Psalm 78:54.

**60** All that is, is God. Just as a wave is not other than the ocean, so creation is not other than the Creator, and God's glory is creation and creation's ability to recognize itself as divine. You are the means for this realization on earth. The world was created for your sake, and you for its sake, and all for the sake of the One Who Is All.

**61** Isaiah 43:7. God's glory is creation. All that is celebrates the One Who Is.

**62** Exodus 15:18. Eternity is not an endless string of time, but the ending of time in the timeless Present.

# Epilogue

Rabbi Chanania ben Akashia teaches,
The Holy Blessed One
wished to confer merit on Israel;
therefore God gave them Torah and
*mitzvot* in abundance,[1]
as it is said,
"*HaShem* desired, for the sake of
 Israel's righteousness,
that the Torah be made great and
 glorious."[2]

**1** This epilogue is from the final teaching in the Mishnah's tractate *Makkot.* It reminds you that your purpose in this world is not simply to know Torah but to be Torah, to engage life through the *mitzvot,* those actions that reveal the union of narrow mind in spacious mind. In this way the universal principle of kindness becomes personal acts of kindness, and the universal principle of justice becomes personal acts of justice. Wisdom that does not transform this world through justice and kindness is false. You can gauge the depth of your wisdom by the just and generous nature of your deeds.

**2** Isaiah 42:21.

# Glossary

***Adam:*** "Earthling," from *adamah*, "earth." "And God said, let us make *adam* ["humanity" in our image, after our likeness] (Genesis 1:26). *Adam* is the way *adamah* becomes conscious of itself as divine.

***Adonai:*** "My Lord." *Adonai* is derived from *adon*, "lord." Since the third century BCE, the Tetragrammaton or four-lettered Name of God (Y-H-V-H) was pronounced as *Adonai* in accordance with the prohibition against actually pronouncing the Tetragrammaton itself.

***Amorah (pl. amoraim):*** Literally "speaker" or "expounder." Derived from the Hebrew *amar*, "to say" or "retell," *amorah* designates the Jewish sages in both Palestine and Babylonia teaching during the period 200CE to 500CE. The *amoraim* primarily expound upon and expand the work of the *tannaim*, the Rabbis whose teachings are codified in the Mishnah.

**Av Bet Din:** "Father of the House of Justice." The *Av Bet Din* was the vice president of the Sanhedrin, the rabbinic court. The *Av Bet Din* presided over the Sanhedrin in the absence of the *Nasi* (literally "prince" and used to designate the president of the Sanhedrin). He was also chief justice of the Sanhedrin when it ruled in criminal cases.

**Avot:** Literally "fathers." *Avot* refers to both the early sages, called fathers, and to the anthology of their teachings, *Pirke Avot,* "Chapters of the Fathers," but often referred to as "Ethics of the Sages."

**Bamot (sing. Bamah):** Literally "high places." *Bamot* are places of worship mentioned in the Bible. I Kings 12:31 notes that Jeroboam I built a *bamah* at both Dan and Bethel.

**Bat Kol:** Literally the "Voice of the Daughter." *Bat Kol* is the term used by the early Rabbis to designate the voice of God. They taught that the *Bat Kol* frequently spoke to the Israelites and that, with the end of the prophetic era, it was through the *Bat Kol* that God continues to instruct the Jews. While referring to God in the masculine, the Rabbis' experience of God's voice and presence (*Shechinah,* also feminine) was clearly feminine. For examples of the *Bat Kol* see *Megillah* 3a, *Taanit* 29a, *Berachot* 17b, *Pesachim* 114a, *Eruvin* 13b and 54b.

**Beraytot:** Rabbinic teachings not found in the Mishnah that are written in the style of the Mishnah. The sixth chapter of *Pirke Avot* is composed of *beraytot.*

**Charut:** "Engraved," from Exodus 32:16. The term is used in association with the tablets of the Ten Commandments written by God. Because the Hebrew Bible is written without vowels, the sages often engage in wordplay by applying a variety of vowel sounds to the consonants of the text to create additional meanings. In this case, *charut* can be read as *cherut,* "freedom," suggesting that God gave the Commandments to free humanity from the yoke of selfishness, ignorance, anger, greed, and violence.

**Chochmah:** Intuitive wisdom, the capacity to know what is *(choah-mah)*. In the Bible *chochmah* is the first of God's creations, through which all the rest was made (Proverbs 8:22ff). In kabbalistic Judaism of the Middle Ages, *chochmah* is imagined as a masculine force coupled with *binah,* rational understanding, his feminine counterpart. The feminine *chochmah* coupled with the feminine *Bat Kol* (God's Voice) and *Shechinah* (God's Presence) suggests strongly that despite their seeming preference for the masculine, the early sages experienced God as feminine.

**Da'at:** Knowledge. Refers to the awareness of the presence of God. In the kabbalistic system, *da'at* emerges when *chochmah,* intuitive wisdom, and *binah,* rational understanding, are in harmony.

**Ehyeh asher Ehyeh:** The Name of God revealed by God to Moses in Exodus 3:14. While often translated as "I am that I am," it is better rendered as "I will be what I will be." The implication is that God is not static and knowable, but fluid and beyond human conceptualization. God does not change, God is change.

**Gehinnom:** The rabbinic name for hell. The name was borrowed from the Valley of the Son of Hinnom (Joshua 15:8) where the refuse of Jerusalem was burned. The Rabbis taught that punishment in Gehinnom lasts up to twelve months, by which time sinners are thought to have repented and gone to heaven.

**Gemara:** From *gamar,* "to complete." Gemara is the rabbinic commentary to the Mishnah, the earliest compilation of rabbinic teaching. The Gemara was composed in Babylonia between 200CE and 500CE. Gemara and Mishnah together compose the Talmud.

**Gerushin:** From *l'garesh,* "to separate." The practice of ceaselessly chanting a Name of God in order to separate oneself from self-centered thoughts and obsessions. Most commonly chanted Names are *HaRachaman* (the Compassionate One) and *Ribbono Shel Olam* (Master of the Universe).

**Halachah:** Refers to the body of Jewish law dealing with both interpersonal relations and obligations to God. Derived from the Hebrew *halakh*, to walk, *halachah* is the way one walks the path of Judaism.

**HaMakom:** Literally, "The Place." *HaMakom* is a rabbinic euphemism for God, the Place in which the world rests, and the Place in which the individual can find comfort.

**HaRachaman:** Literally, "the Compassionate One." Another of the rabbinic Names of God. Compassion in Hebrew, *rachmanut,* comes from the word *rechem,* womb. When we call upon *HaRachaman* we are calling upon God as Mother and hoping to have God feel toward us as a loving mother would toward the child in her womb.

**HaShem:** Literally, "The Name." Given the prohibition against pronouncing the Tetragrammaton, the four-letter Name of God, the sages would often refer to this name as The Name or *HaShem.*

**Koach-mah:** Literally, "what is." A pun on the word *chochmah,* wisdom. One is wise when one knows what is.

**Kohen (pl. Kohanim):** Priestly male descendents of the first priest, Moses's brother, Aaron. The Jewish priesthood is hereditary, coming through the line of the father. Priests perform both ritual and educational functions.

**Makkot:** Literally, "lashes." *Makkot* is the fifth tractate of the order *Nezikin* of the Mishnah, referring to punishments meted out for perjury, manslaughter, and fifty-nine offenses for which the Bible prescribes whipping as the punishment (Numbers 35:9–34; Deuteronomy 19:1–13, 15–21).

**Midrash:** Literally, "expound." Rabbinic commentary on the Bible. There are two types of midrash: *midrash* *halachah,* using the Bible to make points of law, and *midrash aggadah* (story), expanding the biblical narrative with additional stories often with a clear moral message.

**Minyan:** A prayer quorum of ten men in Orthodox Judaism and ten people in liberal Judaism.

**Mishnah:** Literally "teaching" or "instruction." The earliest authoritative collection of rabbinic teaching. An anthology of teachings spanning the period from about 250BCE to 200CE, the Mishnah cites approximately 150 Rabbis.

**Mitzvah (pl. mitzvot):** "Commandment." A religious duty commanded by the Torah or defined by the Rabbis as having biblical origins. Rav, an early third-century sage, taught that the purpose of the commandments *(mitzvot)* is to "refine humanity" (Genesis Rabbah 44:1).

**Mochin d'gadlut:** Literally "big," *gadol,* "brain," *mochin,* but best translated as "spacious mind." It refers to that level of human consciousness that sees all things as manifestations of God. The operative condition of spacious mind is love.

**Mochin d'katnut:** Literally "small," *katan,* "brain," *mochin,* but is best translated as "narrow mind." It refers to that level of human consciousness that focuses on the self and sees everything else as "other." The operative condition of narrow mind is fear.

**Nasi:** Literally "prince." The title given to the president of the Sanhedrin, the rabbinic court. The title was used in this way from the second century BCE through 425CE. As president of the Sanhedrin, the *Nasi* had control of the calendar, established courts throughout the Jewish world, collected money for scholars and academies, and ordained other rabbis. A *Nasi* was addressed as *Rabban,* our Master.

**Olam HaBa:** Literally, "World to Come." In classical rabbinic literature *Olam*

*HaBa* refers to the afterlife. In the context of this translation it refers to the world perceived by *mochin d'gadlut,* spacious mind. This world appears as God manifest, ruled by justice and compassion. The term is used by the Rabbis to refer to the world made perfect through justice and compassion.

**Olam hazeh:** Literally, "this world." In classical rabbinic literature *olam hazeh* refers to the temporal world. In the context of this translation it is understood to refer to the world perceived by *mochin d'katnut,* narrow mind. This world appears as imperfect and struggling toward justice and compassion.

**Omer:** Literally "sheaf." An offering of barley brought to the Temple on the first day of Pesach (Passover).

**Pesach:** Passover, one of the three pilgrimage festivals (the other two are Shavuot and Sukkot) when Jews are required to make sacrifices at the Temple in Jerusalem (Exodus 23:14). Pesach is linked to the lambing season, the barley harvest, and the Exodus from Egypt.

**Pharisees:** The spiritual leaders of the Jewish people during the Second Temple period, 515BCE to 70CE. The Pharisees were a class of scholars focused on expounding the Torah and clarifying the commandments *(mitzvot)*.

**Pirke Avot:** Literally, "Chapters of the Fathers." The ninth tractate of order *Nezikin* in the Mishnah. The "fathers" *(avot)* are the sages cited in the Mishnah. *Pirke Avot* (sometimes called simply *Avot)* contains no halachic (legal) rulings or narrative. It is a collection of ethical sayings, the rabbinic equivalent of both the Book of Proverbs and the Gospel According to Thomas.

**Rabban:** "Our Master." The title given to the *Nasi* or president of the rabbinical court (Sanhedrin).

**Repentir:** Old French meaning "to be sorry." It is the origin of the English word, "repent." The Hebrew equivalent, *teshuvah* (literally, "return"), lacks the emotional focus of both *repentir* and repent, challenging one to change one's behavior for the good regardless of one's sense of guilt or shame.

**Sadducees:** The aristocratic elite associated with the priests during the second half of the Second Temple period, second century BCE through the first century CE. The Sadducees rejected the central tenets of their rivals, the Pharisees: the immortality of the soul and the resurrection of the dead.

**Sanhedrin:** From the Greek, *synedrion,* "sitting in council." The rabbinic court ruled by the *Nasi,* president, and *Av Bet Din,* vice president. While its origin is obscure, rabbinic tradition links the Sanhedrin with the seventy elders chosen by Moses to help rule the people (Numbers 11:4).

**Shabbat:** The Sabbath. The seventh day of the week and a day of rest. Torah says that Shabbat commemorates the culmination of creation (Exodus

20), serves as a sign of the covenant between God and Israel (Exodus 31), and as a reminder of the Jewish people's Exodus from Egypt (Deuteronomy 5).

**Shalem:** "Complete" and "whole."

**Shalom:** "Peace."

**Shamir:** The name given to a worm that, according to rabbinic legend, could eat stone. God created *shamir* to be used to shape the stones of the Temple so they would not be made with tools that could be used as weapons of war.

**Shavuot:** Literally, "Weeks." The second of the three pilgrimage festivals, the other two being Pesach and Sukkot. The name "Weeks" comes from the biblical command to count seven weeks from the time of the Passover harvest, and at that time to commence a second harvest festival (Exodus 34:22; Leviticus 23:15ff; Deuteronomy 16:9–10). Shavuot is also associated with the giving of the Ten Commandments on Mount Sinai.

**Shechinah:** The Presence of God. A distinctly feminine figure, the *Shechinah* is not separate from God, but the way God is experienced in time and space. Coupled with *Bat Kol,* the feminine voice of God (literally, "the Daughter's Voice") and *chochmah,* the feminine Wisdom that was the first of God's creations and the means by which all else was created, *Shechinah* presents a strong case for God as a feminine presence in the lives of the ancient Rabbis.

**Shem Shamayim:** Literally, "Name of Heaven." Refers to God's purpose in creating the world, namely to manifest a level of consciousness that was capable of seeing creation as the Creator manifest in time and space.

**Sheol:** The "abode of the dead." According to the Bible, all people, the good as well as the wicked, go to *Sheol.* **Shlemut:** Derived from *shalem,* wholeness. Nonduality, the realization that God embraces and transcends all things.

**Sh'ma:** Literally, "hearing." The central affirmation of Judaism: "Hear O Israel, Y-H-V-H is our God, Y-H-V-H is One" (Deuteronomy 6:4).

**Sukkot:** Literally, "booths." The third of the three pilgrimage festivals (*Pesach* and *Shavuot* are the other two). Sukkot has both historical and agricultural meaning. Historically it is linked to the forty years of the Israelites' wandering in the Sinai. Agriculturally it is a thanksgiving holiday honoring the gifts of the earth's bounty.

**Tanna (pl. tannaim):** From the Aramaic verb meaning "to study" or "repeat." The *tannaim* were rabbinic sages from 20CE to around 200CE. Over 120 *tannaim* are mentioned in the Mishnah, which is the collection of their teachings and those of their predecessors.

**Tao:** Chinese for "The Way." *Tao* refers to the nature of things and is equivalent to the Hebrew *chochmah* (wisdom) as used in Proverbs: the ordering principle of the universe.

***Tathata:*** Japanese for "suchness." The way things are in and of themselves. To have *chochmah* (wisdom) is to see things as they are *(koach-mah),* i.e. their suchness *(tathata).*

***Teshuvah:*** Literally, "return." *Teshuvah,* though usually translated as "repent," lacks the emotional sense of guilt and remorse associated with that term. To repent one must first have a change of heart. To do *teshuvah,* however, one must simply turn from evil action to good action with or without an accompanying change of heart. Ultimately *teshuvah* is a return to one's true nature as the image and likeness of God, transforming both heart and hand in the service of justice and compassion toward all beings.

***Torah:*** From the Hebrew *yarah,* "to teach." Refers to the Five Books of Moses.

***Torah lishmah:*** Studying Torah for her own sake, the ideal way to study Torah. One studies without ulterior motive, simply for the joy of engaging with God's word.

**Yavneh:** The center of Jewish learning after the destruction of Jerusalem in 70CE.

**Y–H–V–H:** The Tetragrammaton, the four-lettered Name of God. It is a future imperfect form of the Hebrew verb "to be," implying that God is not a static being but being itself: all that is, was, and will be is God.

**Zugot:** Literally, "pairs." Refers to the five pairs of teachers mentioned in the opening chapter of *Pirke Avot*. Tradition holds that the first sage mentioned held the position of *Nasi* (president) while the second held the position of *Av Bet Din* (vice president).

# Suggested Reading

Bunim, Irving. *Ethics from Sinai: A Wide-Ranging Commentary on Pirkei Avos.* New York: Feldheim Publishers, 2000.

Chill, Abraham. *Abravanel on Pirke Avot.* New York: Sepher Hermon Press, 1991.

Goldin, Judah. *Living Talmud: The Wisdom of the Fathers.* New York: Mentor Book, 1964.

Herford, R. Travers. *Pirke Aboth, Ethics of the Talmud: Sayings of the Fathers.* New York: Schocken Books, 1966.

Hertz, Joseph. *Sayings of the Fathers: Pirke Aboth.* New York: Behrman House, 1945.

Hirsch, Samson Raphael. *Chapters of the Fathers.* New York: Feldheim Publishers, 1972.

Kravitz, Leonard, and Kerry Olitzky. *Pirke Avot: A Modern Commentary on*

*Jewish Ethics.* New York: UAHC Press, 1993.

Krupnick, Samson, and Morris Mandel. *Torah Dynamics: Pirkei Avot Looks at Life.* New York: Feldheim Publishers, 1991.

Maimonides, Moses. *Pirkei Avot—Shemoneh Perakim of the Rambam/The Thirteen Principles of Faith.* New York: Moznaim Publishing, 1994.

Marcus, Yosef. *Pirkei Avos: Ethics of the Fathers.* Brooklyn: Merkos L'Inyonei Chinuch, 2005.

Moskowitz, Nachama. *A Bridge to Our Tradition: Pirkei Avot.* New York: UAHC Press, 2001.

Neusner, Jacob. *Judaism and Story: The Evidence of the Fathers According to Rabbi Nathan.* Chicago: University of Chicago Press, 1992.

Pies, Ronald. *The Ethics of the Sages: An Interfaith Commentary on Pirkei*

*Avot.* New Jersey: Jason Aronson, 1999.

Schneersohn, Menachem Mendel. *In the Paths of Our Fathers: Insights into Pirkei Avot from the Works of the Lubavitcher Rebbe.* Brooklyn: Merkos L'Inyonei Chinuch, 1998.

Sforno, Ovadia. *Sforno Commentary on Pirke Avos.* Translated and explanatory notes by Rabbi Raphael Pelcovitz. Brooklyn: Mesorah Publications, 2001.

Shapiro, Rami. *The Divine Feminine in Biblical Wisdom Literature: Selections Annotated and Explained.* Woodstock, VT: SkyLight Paths Publishing, 2005.

_____. *Hasidic Tales: Annotated and Explained.* Woodstock, VT: SkyLight Paths Publishing, 2004.

_____. *The Hebrew Prophets: Selections Annotated and Explained.* Woodstock, VT: SkyLight Paths Publishing, 2004.

_____. *The Sacred Art of Lovingkindness: Preparing to Practice.*

Woodstock, VT: SkyLight Paths Publishing, 2006.

Sicker, Martin. *The Moral Maxims of the Sages of Israel.* iUniverse, 2004.

Stern, Yosef. *Pirkei Avos with Ideas and Insights of the Sfas Emes and Other Chassidic Masters.* Brooklyn: Mesorah Publications, 2004.

Twerski, Abraham, J. *Visions of the Fathers: Pirkei Avos with an Insightful and Inspiring Commentary by Rabbi Abraham J. Twerski, M.D.* Brooklyn: Shaar Press, 2005.

Zlotowitz, Meir. *Pirke Avos, Ethics of the Fathers.* Brooklyn: Mesorah Publications, 2002.

_____. *Pirke Avos Treasury.* Brooklyn: Mesorah Publications, 2000.

## AVAILABLE FROM BETTER BOOKSTORES. TRY YOUR BOOKSTORE FIRST.

## *Sacred Texts*

### JUDAISM

**The Divine Feminine in Biblical Wisdom Literature**
Selections Annotated & Explained
Translation & Annotation by Rabbi Rami Shapiro; Foreword by Rev. Cynthia Bourgeault, PhD
Uses the Hebrew books of Psalms, Proverbs, Song of Songs, Ecclesiastes and Job, Wisdom literature and the Wisdom of Solomon to clarify who Wisdom is.

**Ethics of the Sages:** *Pirke Avot*—Annotated & Explained
Translation & Annotation by Rabbi Rami Shapiro  Clarifies the ethical teachings of the early Rabbis.

**Hasidic Tales:** Annotated & Explained
Translation & Annotation by Rabbi Rami Shapiro; Foreword by Andrew Harvey
Introduces the legendary tales of the impassioned Hasidic rabbis, presenting them as stories rather than as parables.

**The Hebrew Prophets:** Selections Annotated & Explained
Translation & Annotation by Rabbi Rami Shapiro; Foreword by Zalman M. Schachter-Shalomi
Focuses on the central themes covered by all the Hebrew prophets.

**Zohar:** Annotated & Explained   Translation & Annotation by Daniel C. Matt
The best-selling author of *The Essential Kabbalah* brings together in one place the most important teachings of the Zohar, the canonical text of Jewish mystical tradition.

## *Spirituality & Crafts*

**The Knitting Way:** A Guide to Spiritual Self-Discovery
*by Linda Skolnik and Janice MacDaniels*

**The Quilting Path**
A Guide to Spiritual Discovery through Fabric, Thread and Kabbalah
*by Louise Silk*

---

*Or phone, fax, mail or e-mail to:* **SKYLIGHT PATHS** Publishing
Sunset Farm Offices, Route 4 • P.O. Box 237 • Woodstock, Vermont 05091
Tel: (802) 457-4000 • Fax: (802) 457-4004 • www.skylightpaths.com
**Credit card orders:** (800) 962-4544 (8:30AM–5:30PM ET Monday–Friday)
Generous discounts on quantity orders. SATISFACTION GUARANTEED. Prices subject to change.

## Kabbalah from Jewish Lights Publishing

**Awakening to Kabbalah:** The Guiding Light of Spiritual Fulfillment
by Rav Michael Laitman, PhD
**Cast in God's Image:** Discover Your Personality Type Using the Enneagram and Kabbalah
by Rabbi Howard A. Addison
**Ehyeh:** A Kabbalah for Tomorrow  by Dr. Arthur Green

**The Enneagram and Kabbalah, 2nd Edition:** Reading Your Soul
by Rabbi Howard A. Addison
**Finding Joy:** A Practical Spiritual Guide to Happiness  by Dannel I. Schwartz with Mark Hass

**The Gift of Kabbalah:** Discovering the Secrets of Heaven, Renewing Your Life on Earth
by Tamar Frankiel, PhD

**Honey from the Rock:** An Easy Introduction to Jewish Mysticism
by Lawrence Kushner
**Kabbalah:** A Brief Introduction for Christians
by Tamar Frankiel, PhD
**Zohar:** Annotated & Explained  Translation and Annotation by Dr. Daniel C. Matt
Foreword by Andrew Harvey

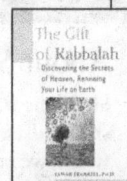

## Judaism / Christianity

**Christians and Jews in Dialogue:** Learning in the Presence of the Other
by Mary C. Boys and Sara S. Lee; Foreword by Dorothy C. Bass
Inspires renewed commitment to dialogue between religious traditions and illuminates how it should happen. Explains the transformative work of creating environments for Jews and Christians to study together and enter the dynamism of the other's religious tradition.

**Healing the Jewish-Christian Rift:**  Growing Beyond Our Wounded History
by Ron Miller and Laura Bernstein; Foreword by Dr. Beatrice Bruteau

**Introducing My Faith and My Community**
The Jewish Outreach Institute Guide for the Christian in a Jewish Interfaith Relationship
by Rabbi Kerry M. Olitzky
**The Jewish Approach to God:** A Brief Introduction for Christians
by Rabbi Neil Gillman
**Jewish Holidays:** A Brief Introduction for Christians
by Rabbi Kerry M. Olitzky and Rabbi Daniel Judson

**Jewish Ritual:** A Brief Introduction for Christians
by Rabbi Kerry M. Olitzky and Rabbi Daniel Judson

**Jewish Spirituality:** A Brief Introduction for Christians
by Rabbi Lawrence Kushner

**A Jewish Understanding of the New Testament**
by Rabbi Samuel Sandmel; new Preface by Rabbi David Sandmel

**We Jews and Jesus**
Exploring Theological Differences for Mutual Understanding
by Rabbi Samuel Sandmel; new Preface by Rabbi David Sandmel  A Classic Reprint
Written in a non-technical way for the layperson, this candid and forthright look at the what and why of the Jewish attitude toward Jesus is a clear and forceful exposition that guides both Christians and Jews in relevant discussion.

**AVAILABLE FROM BETTER BOOKSTORES.
TRY YOUR BOOKSTORE FIRST.**

## About SKYLIGHT PATHS Publishing

SkyLight Paths Publishing is creating a place where people of different spiritual traditions come together for challenge and inspiration, a place where we can help each other understand the mystery that lies at the heart of our existence.

Through spirituality, our religious beliefs are increasingly becoming a part of our lives—rather than *apart* from our lives. While many of us may be more interested than ever in spiritual growth, we may be less firmly planted in traditional religion. Yet, we do want to deepen our relationship to the sacred, to learn from our own as well as from other faith traditions, and to practice in new ways.

SkyLight Paths sees both believers and seekers as a community that increasingly transcends traditional boundaries of religion and denomination—people wanting to learn from each other, *walking together, finding the way.*

For your information and convenience, at the back of this book we have provided a list of other SkyLight Paths books you might find interesting and useful. They cover the following subjects:

| | | |
|---|---|---|
| Buddhism / Zen | Gnosticism | Mysticism |
| Catholicism | Hinduism / | Poetry |
| Children's Books |   Vedanta | Prayer |
| Christianity | Inspiration | Religious Etiquette |
| Comparative | Islam / Sufism | Retirement |
|   Religion | Judaism / Kabbalah / | Spiritual Biography |
| Current Events |   Enneagram | Spiritual Direction |
| Earth-Based | Meditation | Spirituality |
|   Spirituality | Midrash Fiction | Women's Interest |
| Global Spiritual | Monasticism | Worship |
|   Perspectives | | |

*Or phone, fax, mail or e-mail to:* **SKYLIGHT PATHS** Publishing
Sunset Farm Offices, Route 4 • P.O. Box 237 • Woodstock, Vermont 05091
Tel: (802) 457-4000 • Fax: (802) 457-4004 • www.skylightpaths.com
***Credit card orders:*** **(800) 962-4544** (8:30AM–5:30PM ET Monday–Friday)
Generous discounts on quantity orders. SATISFACTION GUARANTEED. Prices subject to change.

**For more information about each book,
visit our website at www.skylightpaths.com**

# The ethical teachings of the rabbinic sages come to life

"When you realize God is all, you engage all as God. You meet each being as a manifestation of the One Being and treat all things with justice, compassion and humility. This is the politics of *Olam* HaBa [the World to Come] that *Pirke Avot* promotes."
—from A Word on Translation

\*\*\*

**SkyLight Illuminations**

Offers today's spiritual seeker an enjoyable entry into the great classic texts of the world's spiritual traditions. Each classic is presented in an accessible translation, with facing pages of guided commentary from experts, offering readers the keys they need to understand the history, context, and meaning of the text. The series enables readers of all backgrounds to experience and understand classic spiritual texts directly, and to make them a part of their lives.

**Also available in the SkyLight Illuminations series:**

***Hasidic Tales:*** *Annotated & Explained* Translation and Annotation by Rabbi Rami Shapiro Foreword by Andrew Harvey

Demonstrates the spiritual power of unabashed joy, offers lessons for leading a holy life and reminds you that the Divine can be found in the everyday.

***The Hebrew Prophets:*** *Selections Annotated & Explained* Translation and Annotation by Rabbi Rami Shapiro Foreword by Zalman M. Schachter-Shalomi

Focuses on the central themes covered by all the prophets: moving from ignorance to wisdom, injustice to justice, cruelty to compassion and despair to joy.

**Zohar:** *Annotated & Explained* Translation and Annotation by Daniel C. Matt Foreword by Andrew Harvey

Explains references and mystical symbols in the canonical text of Kabbalah and clarifies its bold claim: We have always been taught that we need God, but in order to manifest in the world, God needs us.

\*\*\*

For more information about these and other SkyLight Paths books, please visit our website, www.skylightpaths.com

**Rabbi Rami Shapiro** is an award-winning storyteller, poet, and essayist, and director of the Simply Jewish Foundation. He is the author of *Minyan: Ten Principles for Living a Life of Integrity* (Bell Tower); *Hasidic Tales: Annotated and Explained; The Hebrew Prophets: Selections Annotated and Explained; The Divine Feminine in Biblical Wisdom Literature: Selections Annotated and Explained;* and *The Sacred Art of Lovingkindness: Preparing to Practice* (all SkyLight Paths) and other books.

**Praise for Rabbi Rami Shapiro's Work**

"One of the outstanding leaders in the field of modern spirituality.... His mastery of English and Hebrew enables him to render the ancient words in ways that bring light and inspiration."

—*Jewish Media Review*

"Rami Shapiro has given us two gifts, an illuminating contemporary

rendering of this timeless spiritual classic, along with commentary of everyday, personal stories that reveal the joy-filled wisdom. I loved it!"
—**Sylvia Boorstein,** author of *That's Funny, You Don't Look Buddhist*

"Powerful and rich ... written so skillfully and accessibly that it will be read by peoples from all traditions. Opens for us the great beauty and necessity of kindness in the world today."
—**Roshi Joan Halifax,** abbot, Upaya Zen Center

## Also by Rabbi Rami Shapiro

### The Sacred Art of Lovingkindness
***Preparing to Practice***
Explores Judaism's Thirteen Attributes of Lovingkindness as the

framework for cultivating a life of goodness. Shapiro translates these attributes into practices—drawn from the teachings of a variety of faith traditions—that allow you to actualize God's glory through personal deeds of lovingkindness. With a foreword by Marcia Fordd.

*Walking Together, Finding the Way®*

**SKYLIGHT PATHS®**
PUBLISHING

Sunset Farm Offices, Route 4, P.O. Box 237
Woodstock, VT 05091
Tel: (802) 457-4000  Fax: (802) 457-4004

www.skylightpaths.com

# Back Cover Material

**The clear and compelling wisdom of the rabbinic sages can become a companion for your own spiritual journey.**

At the heart of Judaism is an ethical imperative to live life from your true self, as the image and likeness of God. To do this, you must see the greatness of God manifest in all things, and therefore engage each moment with grace, humility, and justice. This imperative flowers in the words of the early Rabbis (250BCE-250CE), who captured God's call to be holy in *Pirke Avot,* a collection of pithy sayings on how best to live an ethical life.

This engaging introduction to the wisdom sayings of the rabbinic sages puts you in direct conversation with them, allowing the sages to speak directly to you about what matters in life and how to live it with dignity. With fresh, contemporary translation and provocative commentary, Rabbi Rami Shapiro focuses on the central themes in this Jewish wisdom compendium—study, kindness, compassion. He clarifies the rabbinic proverbs and parables in order to expose the ethical principles at their root. By recalling the ancient voices of the rabbinic sages, he shows us the contemporary significance of their timeless wisdom and distills *Pirke Avot* not as a book about ethics but as a practical guide to living ethically today.

Now you can experience the wisdom of the early Rabbis even if you have no previous knowledge of Judaism or rabbinic literature. This SkyLight Illuminations edition presents the ethical teachings of the rabbinic sages, with insightful yet unobtrusive commentary that conveys *Pirke Avot's* core challenge of God to the Jewish people, and through them all humanity: We are to be holy as God is holy. We are to be, in a human way, what God is in a divine way.

***

"Captures the holy essence of each word while it mines lessons for sacred daily living.... Raises this classic of

rabbinic literature simultaneously to new heights and new depths. For this work alone, Rabbi Shapiro will be named one of the great teachers of the twenty-first century."
—**Rabbi Kerry M. Olitzky,** executive director, Jewish Outreach Institute; coeditor, *Pirke Avot: A Modern Commentary on Jewish Ethics*

"A fresh translation and a contemporary, often innovative commentary and application of an age-old source of Jewish wisdom."
—**Rabbi Elliot N. Dorff,** author, *The Way Into* Tikkun Olam *(Repairing the World)*

www.ingramcontent.com/pod-product-compliance
Lightning Source LLC
Chambersburg PA
CBHW011717220426
43662CB00018B/2401